Books by Dav(

<> <> <

Truth be Told: A journey from the dark side of OCD

The Little Book of OCD

Truth Be Told

A journey from the dark side of OCD

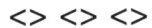

<> <> <>

Dave Preston

Published by Dave Preston

© Copyright 2016 Dave Preston

All rights reserved. No part of this book may be reproduced, scanned or distributed, in any printed or electronic form, without permission. Please do not participate in or encourage piracy of copyrighted materials in violation of the author's rights. Purchase only authorized editions.

Biography (Non-fiction)
Health & Wellness – Psychology – Obsessive Compulsive Disorder

10 9 8 7 6 5 4 3 2 1

Designed by Dave Preston

Publisher's Note:
This book is a work of non-fiction. The names of some characters in the book have been changed to protect their real identities.

To my wife and best friend, Jackie.

Thank you for leaving the porch light on.

<> <> <>

Special thanks to:

My wife Jackie for her love and support and acting as a sounding board as I took the journey to write this book.

My sons Garrett and Aaron for their love and support.

My sister Barb for being there and all the fantastic editing work she did.

My sister Janet for reading the draft and offering feedback.

This book was truly a family affair.

Andrew for reading the draft, offering feedback and having enough faith in me to offer to make a movie based on the book.

Part One
<> <> <>
Predicament

Chapter 1
Into the Ashes

The fire left a blackened landscape when it swept through the Trepanier Valley in the waning days of summer, 2012. Born from an unknown cause, high winds pushed the raging fire into Peachland, destroying four homes in the process and leading to the evacuation of 1,500 scared residents.

Spurred on by the wind, the fire quickly blew across the bench that is the rural area called Trepanier and into the gorge carved out by Trepanier Creek. There it attacked trees by the hundreds and ravaged the ground cover of Ponderosa pine needles and other forest debris.

The fire's wake left a blackened scar. Soon winter snow covered the scar. The following spring nature provided a flush of new growth. Segmented snake grass, common around creeks, rivers and lakeshores in the southern interior of British Columbia, grew tall and proud in the ashes of the fire. Tiny bushes tentatively grasped for purchase in the rocky slopes of the Trepanier Gorge. Many kinds of grass grabbed a foothold in the ash.

Two hundred feet below the walking trail that runs from the elementary school to the Trepanier Bench, a solitary pine had succumbed to the previous fall's raging fire. The tree split in two. The top half split off from its trunk, falling haphazardly on top of other trees on the slope of the gorge. The bottom half fell too, in the opposite direction, its top landing near the cold water of the creek, its bottom pointing up toward the trail above.

Fire had razed the section of tree near the creek. What little bark remained on the outside was black as coal. When the tree toppled over, a hollowed out section ended up facing the blackened earth underneath.

Scoured out by high temperature flames, the inside of the tree was blackened. To smell it would be to smell a large campfire that had burned for hours, only to be doused with water. It smelled like a mixture of burnt wood, humidity and the death of a living thing. The hollowed portion resembled a scorched coffin, just big enough for a man to squeeze in.

I crawled inside the blackened tomb, laying half in and half out. The hollowed out section narrowed at its far end and I could wrestle in no more. It was June 27, 2013. I had a pack of cigarettes, a lighter, a Mars bar and a knife.

It seemed to be a good place to die.

Outside the temperature is frigid and crisp. It's a sunny Sunday afternoon. In Alberta, the sun blazes fiercely when the air temperature reaches that of a walk-in freezer. It gets so cold in northern Alberta in January that the sky refuses to snow, though right now there is plenty of the white stuff packed hard on roads and piled high next to curbs.

Mom is out in the living room, likely reading an Ellery Queen or Alfred Hitchcock mystery digest. She reads voraciously. I often walk to the corner store a block from our house to buy the books for her. If there's change left over, I happily spend it on two-for-a-penny candy or a bag of chips.

Three of my brothers and sisters live on their own. One brother and one sister live with mom, dad and I. My siblings at home are in high school. I started junior high and I'm getting used to being in Grade 6 – the lowest level of my four-grade school.

Dad is driving to some meeting or lecture in a town several hours away. Prior to leaving, he sits down with me on the couch and we discuss fitting in at school. Some of the cooler, bigger kids are bringing knives to school, mostly of the pocket variety. They are pressuring me to be like them but I don't want to.

A few months before I had been an air force Base Brat. Dad retired from the armed forces and we moved the whole two miles to town. I went from Base Brat to Towney and I sure don't want to be one of the tough, knife-carrying Towneys.

"Don't let anyone make you do something you don't want to," my dad says.

Up to that point, dad was more a father than a dad and the talk on the couch of our Towney house is a singular moment of advice from dad to son. It is a moment to be cherished and, as it turns out, never to be repeated.

Our house is small, barely 900 square feet and half of

that is frigid basement. I'm in my small bedroom upstairs, not 10 feet on a side. A single bed occupies most of the space and the family electric organ sits shoehorned against one wall.

I'm 11 and I'm no pianist. Most of the time I play two-handed, one set of fingers pressing the chord buttons and the other plunking out the melody. I spend hours hammering out 'Moon River' or 'Green Sleeves'. My personal favourite is the only song I can play with both hands on the keys, 'Nadia's Theme', the haunting theme to a recently started soap opera called The Young and the Restless. With the organ blaring out song after song, I'm oblivious to goings on elsewhere in the house. As far as I'm concerned, all is quiet. Because of the music, I can't hear people outside my room.

Mom opens my door. The look on her face shocks me into inaction. I freeze trying to read what the crimson color on her face means and why tears are burrowing furrows into her cheeks. Her face looks like a horrid Halloween mask, painfully contorted and most inhuman.

"David, your daddy's dead."

My heart sinks into the pit of my stomach. A cold sweat envelops me and shaking begins somewhere near my toes, rising quickly through my limbs and torso.

I take solace in my pillow. I cry a little. Mostly I am bewildered at how my life has suddenly changed from a happy Sunday afternoon of song playing to something foreign and uncertain. I barely know my dad as a dad and here my mom has told me that he was swept from this world.

More than an hour passes. I venture out to the living room to find my brother and sister, my mom and some family friends sobbing in individual sorrow. I sit in the gold cloth-covered armchair and watch the unfamiliar scene of grief unfold.

Dad always drove fast, too fast. I don't know if speed is a factor in his death. I'm told he hit a patch of black ice on the asphalt highway, slid and slammed head-on into an oncoming gravel truck. He died instantly.

We are not a touchy, feely family. The grief we feel is solitary in nature, not outwardly shared. I cry far too little for an 11-year-old boy.

Lying half in and half out of the burnt tree, I thought about my dad, his death in that cold winter and what effect that had on my life.

Something changed the day my dad died and it solidified over the coming weeks. Instead of shedding tears, I shed my boyhood and my innocence.

At the funeral I told my family, gathered around, "It's done and over with. We have to get on with life." I'm sure my mom and siblings thought it a very mature thing for a kid to say but looking back, I know it was a sign that I wasn't dealing with my dad's death well at all. I needed help but there was no help forthcoming.

If ever there was a time I needed a dad, it was then in the long winter of 1974/75. I found myself lost, suffering from the loss of my dad. I didn't know how to deal with it; we had moved to town (as foreign a place from the air force base where I had grown up as Timbuktu) and something was going on inside my head.

Walking aimlessly along the Trepanier Gorge trail minutes before, my intention was to find a quiet place to die. I bought the knife specifically for that reason but once I found nature's blackened casket, and even though I had unfolded the knife and laid it on my chest, I was drawn toward remembering my past.

Perhaps that's what people about to die by suicide do. They spend time thinking about their past, analyzing what was and what could have been, before they take a short-bladed knife and plunge it in their heart or slash strongly at their wrists. (I hadn't decided yet which way I was going to end my life.)

I know why my thoughts were drawn to my dad on that cool, summer afternoon. It's not just because he died and that left a hole in my being. It was because his death was the beginning of all that was wrong and twisted, bizarre and awful that became a big part of my life. What happened a few hours before that forced me to the hollowed out log miles from my home all began on a freezing winter day in 1975.

My family loved me, or at least had loved me up until a few hours before. As I lay in the log and listened to the sound of raindrops pattering on leaves and rocks, I thought a lot about my two boys and my wife. I was sure at this lowest of low points in my scarred life that they were even now abandoning me and withdrawing their love for me.

I had done something monstrous, inexcusable. I certainly couldn't excuse my behaviour or find it inside me to forgive myself. What I had done, the torment I had thrown my family into, was unforgiveable. Also not forgivable were the thoughts that had become a part of me and shaped who I had become. Since shortly after my dad died on a frozen northern Alberta road, I had been tormented by thoughts that had become a big part of who I was.

As I lay mostly inside the burned out log, I thought how

my life had changed drastically because of the thoughts.

I was sick. I was a pervert. I was probably a sociopath, maybe a psychopath. There was no way of getting around the conclusions I had drawn a thousand times before and reaffirmed on that dreary June day. As I inhaled the smell of burnt forest and trembled from the cold and fear, I told myself I was a sick bastard who deserved to be alone under a log with a knife.

Tears did not come in the burned forest. There were times I would let out a snort of sadness to the breeze but, strangely, I either couldn't cry or wouldn't cry. My emotions were wrought with sadness, I felt – no I knew, my life was over, but I did not cry.

Every mistake I ever made, every time I went left when I should have gone right, flooded into my brain. I stared up at the black carcass of the tree and watched as my life's mistakes replayed before me.

I felt bad for my wife and kids and my siblings. I wasn't thinking about them missing me right then. I was thinking about the disgrace I had brought upon my family and how utterly screwed up I had made their lives. They would be lost, much like me. I hoped beyond hope they would be able to find it within themselves to forget about me, and forge on in a new life without the deviant I was.

Just days after my dad's funeral I return to school and throw myself at schoolwork. Something takes hold of me and I begin to excel at social studies, math and science. I will go on to win half the year-end medals handed out to scholastic achievers. The knife-carrying Towneys back off on their harsh demands that I carry a knife, perhaps out of pity for me losing my dad to an icy Alberta road. Most of my teachers look upon me differently when I return to school, doling out extra doses of kindness and understanding.

I start to get along with the kids my age and I'm invited several times to the well-known parties at Megan's house. Megan's family lives on an acreage several miles outside town. To be invited to her house for a Saturday night party is the pinnacle of Grade 6 life. Sound system in the corner, mood lights in the basement, punch made by Megan's mom and the promise of kissing in the corner all make a party at Megan's the highlight of the school year.

Put a bunch of 11 and 12-year-olds in a dimly lit basement, unsupervised, and nature will take its course. I'm sure there is more than kissing going on in the beanbag chairs that sit like warm clouds on the basement floor. For the most part, I'm far too shy to partake in lip smacking. Not to mention things aren't going so great in my mind.

Junior high is a time of blooming sexuality, feet tripping over thin air, very close friendships, dances in the school gym and feeling the wind whip by my ears while riding a bike. I think it's supposed to be a carefree, adventurous time, but for me it is a time of wonderment, loss and worry.

I've always been an anxious person. As long as I can remember, life has been a journey from one anxious moment to the next. Rarely a day would go by when anxiety didn't show itself in some way. Sometimes it was a little nervous feeling. Other times the anxiety made my body ache. The worst kind of anxiety I felt was a panic attack. When I was young, I didn't understand what a panic attack was but I sure knew what it felt like.

A panic attack was what I was having the day in June 2013 when I lay in the burned out log and contemplated my life and my impending death. It was incredibly difficult to focus. It's as if my whole body was wrapped in a cloak of extreme anxiety. My breathing was shallow and laboured. My eyes were wide and I noticed every little sound in the forest, be it a squirrel rustling a leaf or the sound of rain splattering on the surface of the creek a few metres away. I felt pins and needles in my skin. It was cool out but I was sweating. I was fully aware of every part of my body. I could sense my toes, my ears, the ends of my fingertips.

Though I thought a lot about my past and what brought me to be alone beside the creek on an overcast day, I had difficulty even thinking. It was as if I had to force the thoughts out of my head because it was stuffed with cotton batting.

I examined the knife several times, twisting it around, looking at the four-inch blade, the glint of the stainless steel, the sharp edge along one side. I turned the knife over and over. There was little feeling associated with looking at the knife, my chosen way to leave this life. I was detached from the implement of my demise, yet I twirled it nonetheless, as I tried to remember points in my life when things had gone wrong.

It was rare for me to have a full-blown panic attack. Then again, I had never been in trouble or faced the end of my life like that day. I was used to feeling anxious, but not overly used to having it reach panic stage.

I had thought about suicide before. Many times. Perhaps hundreds of times. I'd just thought about it, wondering if it was the solution to a mind gone mad. I had never come up with a plan before, never assembled the required equipment to carry out the act.

Part of me wanted to scream at the birds above me, "Why did it have to come to this?" Part of me wanted to cry. I thought I was a bad person the world would be better off without having. I thought about my past.

Brent is tall and lanky. His bedroom is small, like mine, but it's special. It's painted black as night. It's the coolest preteen room in town. Sitting next to the window on a stand are three floodlights, blue, red, green. There's a switch contraption we wired to turn the lights on and off to the sound of a good beat.

Brent has a stereo and a collection of LPs. We rock out in his room. April Wine's 'Oowatanite', 'Lady' by Styx. Anything by Bachman Turner Overdrive. It is 1976, the rock is pure and jeans are tight. There's nothing else to do in this town. Rocking out in Brent's room is about the best thing there is.

It's getting on to suppertime. I say I had better go. I slip out the side door to the driveway. I get on my 10-speed bike and start pedalling away. No more than 100 yards from Brent's a thought pops into my head. *Something bad is going to happen.*

It's not just a thought. It's a whisper. It's a thought and a feeling, like a sense of dread, a sense of foreboding. My brain is a crystal ball and I've suddenly foretold the immediate future. *Something bad is going to happen.*

I screech to a stop. One foot rests on a pedal, the other sits on the ground. I twist my head around and look back at Brent's house. *Something bad is going to happen. Something bad is going to happen. Something bad is go...*

It's like a litany now. *I have to go back. I have to go back and check because something is happening, something bad. Something bad is happening and I know it, I can feel it, it's something bad.*

I scrunch up my nose. I breathe shallowly. A tingling runs up my spine, from my butt to way under my scalp. The thought is small, tentative, poking around inside my head as I straddle my bike in the middle of the street.

Something bad is going to happen. Or it's happening right now or it's already happened. Could it have happened already? Has it already happened? Something bad has happened, is happening or will happen. Something bad. Where's this thought coming from? What does it mean? There's no reason for thinking what I'm thinking. But maybe there is a reason for it. Maybe it's because something bad has happened. I have to go back. I have to go check.

When I left, Brent was okay. His mom was okay. His mom was stirring something in a pot in the kitchen. There was no danger. Nothing should be happening.

I can't go home. I can't go home if I don't know. I need to know. I need to know that Brent is safe. I need to know his mom is safe. They're in the house and they were safe but now they may not be safe and I have to check.

The thought is louder now. I crane my neck and stare at the house. I look to see if anything is amiss. Part of me knows I'm going to be late for my own supper. Part of me is being pulled back to the house I came from.

Going back would be stupid. There's no reason to go back. Brent is fine. But what if he's not? What if some bad thing did happen and Brent is not fine and he's hurt or there's a problem. There could be a fire. I don't see smoke.

There's no fire. But there's something wrong. I can feel it.

I start to pant. My palms are sweaty.

What's going on? I don't know this thought. I don't want to know this thought. Where is it coming from? It wasn't there and then it was there, pulling me. I want to go back and see Brent. Mom will be mad if I'm late for supper. I have to go but something could be happening. Something could be going on. I really should go back, or should I?

I hear only the distant sound of traffic on the highway and the rustle of leaves in trees that dot the lawns around me. A dog barks in the distance. Things are getting muffled. I don't know what's going on. The thought is stuck in my head.

Something bad is going to happen. I should go back to see if Brent is all right. He's my friend, I like him a lot, and I really need to know if everything is okay or if something has happened or maybe it's happening right now.

I shuffle my foot on the gravel of the roadway. I hesitantly turn my bike back toward Brent's house. I don't know why I'm going. I don't know what I expect to find. I feel panicky. I feel like I'm going to throw up. I'm panting and the thought won't go away.

Something bad is going to happen.

I pedal slowly. I don't want anyone to see me. They'll think I'm a freak or a dweeb. I'm trying to fit in at school and the last thing I want someone to think about me is that I'm a dweeb. I feel my heart beating in my chest. There's a throbbing in my ears. I pull up to the front of the house. I straddle my bike.

Why am I back here? Nothing has shown me that anything at all wrong is going on. Here I am, back again. I'm starting to sweat and I think I might pee my pants.

Something bad is going to happen or is happening but I don't see anything. I must be going crazy.

Brent's mom looms in the picture window. She crosses the living room into the kitchen.

She's okay. She's walking, she's there, and everything.

Suddenly the thought isn't there anymore. I feel very stupid. I'm supposed to be going home. I spy Brent through the window. He's in the kitchen. I can tell he's talking to his mom.

It's so stupid to be here.

I whip my bike around and pedal hard for home. I get to the nearest intersection. I laugh at myself for being a dweeb. A thought pops into my head.

Something bad is going to happen.

If I came to the creek-side burned out log to kill myself, I wasn't doing a very good job of it. I alternately held the knife and set it down on the damp ground. I chain smoked cigarettes and, at one point, attempted to eat the Mars bar that had been smashed in my back jeans pocket. It was a gooey mess.

I continued to think about how twisted and insane my life had become. My thoughts turned to several hours before and what pre-empted my day and sent me into the forest with a knife.

It was a normal June morning. My wife Jackie was upstairs in the bathroom of our town home, having a shower and performing her morning ritual before work. I was in the back yard, the Oasis, as Jackie had come to calling it.

That spring, my son Aaron and I had spent hours fixing up the back yard. A concrete pad extended from the back of the house into the yard. We used to have an outdoor table, six chairs and an umbrella on the pad, which was far too small. It was difficult to get into the chairs next to the house and the back legs of the far chairs inevitably ended up in the grass. Aaron and I changed that by extending the patio with wide, stone pavers.

Jackie's mom, the last of our parents to be alive, died in an Edmonton nursing home the previous year. That spring Jackie received her share of the inheritance and, in addition to paying off a mountain of bills, we decided to purchase new outdoor furniture for the newly extended patio.

We spent a lot of time fixing up the back yard into the Oasis. A garden at the back sported a large spruce tree, an enormous Hosta and a collection of brightly coloured snapdragons. Two armchairs, a loveseat, a coffee table and a small canopy sat on the patio, surrounded by four black plastic urns sporting flowers.

That morning I sat in the Oasis, having my morning smoke and drinking my first cup of coffee of the day. It was shortly before 9 a.m. The sun was up, though it promised to be cloudy for much of the day with the strong chance of showers.

A vehicle pulled up on the street behind our house. I could see through the gaps in the back fence that the vehicle had pulled up on an angle, half way covering the driveway where our car sat. A few moments later, the gate swung open.

Two young police officers stood in the gateway, one male and one female. Both wore street clothes and bulletproof vests. The female officer saw me sitting on an armchair and said, "Mr. Preston?"

I said, "Yes," and began to rise.

She motioned me over and said to me words that changed my life in far more ways than I would have thought possible. "We're here as part of a child pornography investigation."

There are four naked kids in the dugout.

Canadian Forces Base Cold Lake is divided into four residential neighbourhoods. To get to Mackenzie, you drive through the front gate and hang an immediate right, taking the road down the small valley carved out by the creek then up the other side.

The road turns left and then the elementary school is on the right. Behind the school are a field and what local kids call the Big Woods. Between those woods and the school are two baseball diamonds.

Each of the diamonds has two dugouts. They're called that because they're dug out of the ground. The side facing the ball diamond is covered with chain link fencing. The other three sides are covered in plywood. A doorway is cut out of one end and anyone entering it has to walk down three or four steps to get to the dirt floor of the dugout.

There are four of us that live in two duplexes across from the school. Two boys, two girls. We have been the best of friends long before we started Grade 1. We play a lot in the field behind the school, venturing into the Big Woods and often ending up in one particular dugout – the one farthest away from our houses.

Kids of all ages hang out around the dugouts. Many use them as an emergency bathroom. On warm summer days, the dirt floors of the dugouts exude a terrible smell from who knows how much kid pee.

We go in the dugout and we play around. Many times

the playing involves taking our clothes off. We touch each other. We imitate sex, though we have no clue what sex is. Body parts touch body parts on the dirt floor.

It happens more than a few times. We treat it as a big secret.

Later on, as I grew up, I kept thinking back to the dugout. I got an uneasy feeling each time. It bothered me what we did in the dugout. How did we four youngsters know to imitate sexual acts with each other? Did we learn them from someone? I tried many times to remember as I grew up but I couldn't remember.

Now and again, I think about the dugout and although I can't actually remember with any certainty, I have the sense that someone else was in that dugout with us. Someone older. Four decades later, I still can't remember there being a teenager or adult in the dugout with us, but thinking about that dank, dark hole in the ground still makes me uneasy.

Chapter 2
The Porch Light

Child pornography. The words shocked me. Fear gripped me. I sweated profusely and it seemed the world swirled before my eyes. Another officer approached me and spoke with a soothing voice. The officer took me back into the carport and said something about a search warrant and that I would not be allowed back in the house until the investigation was over.

I wanted to cry. I wanted to die. A thousand different thoughts hit my brain all at once. I was overloaded. I stood in the carport shaking, trying desperately to get a smoke out of my pack and light it.

Officers were inside my house, inside my domain. I could see them, through the back door and gate. They came through the front door. I had no idea how many officers there were in total.

"You are not being detained. You are not under arrest. You are free to go at any time," the officer said.

Standing in the carport, I saw Jackie and my son Aaron come out of the house. The cops had woken Aaron up, hours earlier than he was used to. Sleepily he trudged into the back yard.

"What is going on?" Jackie asked, a look of horror on her face.

"I don't know," I mouthed. I knew.

I paced between the carport and the parking spots behind the back fence. I smoked and stood in place, lost. I wore a T-shirt, a worn pair of jeans and a pair of holey-sole shoes. The panic attack started as I stood there behind my house. It came fast like a hit upside the head from a baseball bat.

The officer reiterated that I was not under arrest, not being detained and was free to go. He asked if I wanted to go out for a coffee. He said I could come back in a few hours when his fellow officers were done their investigation. I asked him if he could get my wallet or at least my bankcard from it. He said sure and walked toward the house.

Another officer, the only one dressed in his RCMP uniform, tried to strike up a conversation. He said he wasn't part of the investigation, He was there, with a marked police car, because sometimes undercover cops show up at places where there was a drug house and the people inside might think the plainclothes officers were rival gang members intent on ripping off the drug house occupants.

I mumbled a few words to the uniformed officer and soon enough the other officer showed up with my bankcard. By that time, I was completely lost, not thinking clearly at all and swamped with raw emotions and a million thoughts. A part of me wanted to walk into the back yard and hug Jackie and Aaron. I needed support but I didn't feel I deserved it.

I knew my life as I knew it was over. I started walking. A half a block from our house was a small coffee shop and bakery and I found myself standing in line. When it came to my turn, I asked for a large dark roast. I paid and added cream at a small side table. I walked out to the front of the bakery.

Instead of turning left to go back home, I turned right and sat on a public bench. The view of Okanagan Lake was spectacular, but it was lost in a haze of muddled thoughts and wrenched feelings inside me. From my vantage point, I could see the front of my house. There were several cars parked in front but no marked police cruisers.

I sat on the bench sipping coffee. At some point, I stood up and continued to the right, away from my home. At first, I was thinking about taking a walk, maybe a block or so. I walked to the end of the block and turned right. I walked further and took another right.

My heart pounded in my chest. I broke out in a cold sweat. My breathing was fast and shallow.

I kept walking. I didn't feel like I was walking away from something but rather walking toward something. I desperately wanted to be alone with my thoughts. I couldn't stand to be in the company of anyone. I continued to walk past my house a block away until I reached the pedestrian crossing on the highway.

Waiting for the walk signal to change I felt like I was in a daze, a thick fog. I crossed the highway and walked to the convenience store on the corner. I couldn't imagine what I looked like. Could anyone be able to tell I was in trouble by the look on my face? I bought a Mars bar and two packs of smokes.

Turning right out of the convenience store, I slowly walked across the parking lot of the mall. I was walking toward the road that led to the school but at the last moment, I turned and walked to the dollar store.

The aisles of the store were crammed with knick-knacks and cheap household items. I looked around for some rope but couldn't find what I was looking for. Drawing near to the front counter, I spied a collection of knives in a basket below the cash register. I picked up a folding knife and placed it on the counter.

Ten minutes later, I found myself behind the elementary school near the old house. A stark concrete foundation was all that was left of the old place and it looked even drearier filled with weeds as tall as I, and garbage. It was a place where local kids hung out. The trails in the area were popular with kids who owned BMX bikes.

I continued walking and crested a hill. I sat down in the peace of the forest and hoped no one out for a walk would come across me.

Child pornography. The words filled me with dread. What must Jackie and Aaron have thought when they heard those words? What of my other son Garrett, living at my sister's home in Lethbridge? What of my sister, my other sister or my three brothers? What would people in town think when they heard? Surely, they would hear. Regardless how well-known I was they would abandon me, I was sure. They would look upon me with scorn and derision and spit at my feet.

I could hear noises in the forest and far off traffic on the highway. I stood up and crested a small hill, finding the trail that wound along the top of the Trepanier Gorge to the Trepanier Bench.

Walking along the trail, I could begin to smell the remnants of the previous fall's raging fire. In a few places, I could see where the grass and forest floor debris had burned through as the fire raced up the side of the gorge. Everywhere there was new growth but the smell of burnt forest rose from the ashes under the grass and small bushes.

I continued to walk along the trail until I could no longer hear traffic noise. I could only hear the sounds of the forest. I was well and truly alone but too close to the trail. The thought of someone I knew sauntering down the trail, bumping into me and asking me how things were going was unbearable.

Turning right, I peered over the edge and down the sharply angled gorge side. No one could see me down there. I descended.

I learned quickly that wet charcoal encrusted ground is slick. I slid in many places, my holey-soles filling quickly with a kind of black muck that stuck to my bare feet. I grabbed at branches and bushes as I half stepped, half slid down the slope. The further I got the louder Trepanier Creek became. I could hear it gurgling and sloughing off rocks on its way through the gorge to Okanagan Lake.

After about 10 minutes of mostly skidding down the embankment, I found myself on a flat bench a few metres away from the creek. I looked around. Tall trees, some burned beyond recognition, some still standing proud, poked into the sky around me. The creek gurgled along; the odd bird sang a short tune. It was quiet and I was alone.

I sat on the ground. My jeans were caked with the black fire muck. Black handprints were all over my T-shirt. I looked a mess. I felt a mess. I felt truly alone. That's when I saw the burned out log, about 10 metres away.

It began to rain, a slight, drizzling June rain that cooled the air and dampened sound. Tired from the exertion of getting to the creek and from the stress of the past hour, I approached the log. I peered underneath and saw the hollowed out section underneath. I first lay under the log then slowly slithered my legs inside. It felt like a dark, cold crypt.

Never before in my life had I felt so alone. My mind drifted to the past.

When the thoughts exactly started, I do not know. I'm not even sure they did start -- at least in the sense that they weren't there and then suddenly they were there.

I have no recollection of them before my dad's car careened into the gravel truck, but I do recall instances, some blurry, some sharp, of thoughts gone awry while I was in Grade 6.

It's not like one day this big, bad thing showed up and my mind was wracked with grief. The thoughts slowly evolved, showing up at some point as an indistinguishable problem. Then they morphed inside my head, not at any great pace but ploddingly, with purpose.

It was like catching one of those awful winter colds a kid gets at least twice a year after the temperature plummets for the season. One moment he's fine and the next there's this feeling like something isn't quite right but he's not sure what's wrong, just that there is something a bit off. Maybe he sniffs but it's not a big enough sniff to be a cold sniff, but it's there all the same. He's headed toward getting sick but he's not aware he's getting sick. Things aren't as peachy keen as they were 10 minutes before.

This was no cold. This was something going on inside my head. It was so slowly insidious I had no clue anything was the matter before it was too late. There were no signs like when you get a cold and maybe you start sneezing at a regular rate, then you get snot running down your top lip and then there's a tickle at the back of your throat. This thing began its work as quiet as an altar boy on Sunday morning. It didn't just appear in my head. It slithered in like a snake.

I am absolutely positively sure puberty had something to do with it. If not, the timing was impeccable. My body was changing faster than a waxed sled rocketing down a snow-covered Suicide Hill in February. With the physical change my emotions were running amok, my feelings bounced from elation to despair in a blink of an eye and girls began to change from being something icky to something nice.

Everything about me, like every other 12-year-old kid in Grand Centre Junior High School, was changing at lightning speed and, in my case, so was my mind. Not in the sense of a maturing brain heading toward adulthood, but in the sense that something totally screwed up was brewing and it happened to be going on when my body and emotions were in turmoil.

In the beginning, the changes in my mind were one more change in the overall puberty scheme of things. I had no idea that the thoughts I was having, and the emotions that went along with them, were anything but perfectly normal. At 12, I was as liable to cry watching a Disney movie as yell at my mom for some perceived motherly transgression.

The thoughts I was having were another unexplainable facet of growing up. Or so I thought.

I know exactly what my mom would have said had she known about what was going on in my brain in those early days: "Quit worrying." It would be the exact mom thing for her to say and, really, it was all about worrying, at least early on. I sure didn't know it was going to change into something else.

I lost track of time inside my carbon coffin. My mind bounced between being numb and thoughtless to thinking about the past and present. I didn't know exactly why the police had shown up at my house that morning. I suspected it had something to do with chatting on the Internet and that was bad enough.

It was a secret part of my life. It was disgusting and mean, inexplicable and dangerous. It mirrored thoughts I had for many, many years. I knew, regardless the demeanour I portrayed to my family and the rest of the world, that I was a sick, twisted bastard for what I thought and what I expressed on the Internet.

I imagined Jackie was now fully aware of my misdeeds, having been informed by the police who were rifling through our private lives. My actions had led to a mind-blowing disruption of the lives of my wife and son. Relegated to the back yard, they would not be allowed back in the house until the police were finished.

At some point, as the rain continued to dribble onto the ground around me, I succumbed to the stress of the moment. The day became more than I could handle and, holding onto the small folding knife, I succumbed to sleep.

I don't know how long I slept but I awoke with the stark

realization that I had to go to the bathroom and not for a pee. Not an outdoorsman, it took me a while to figure out what generations of people had long since figured out, how to take a shit in the woods. That duty accomplished, I sat on the ground and watched the creek slosh by me.

So alone. I was not only by myself in the woods but I couldn't communicate with anyone even if I wanted to. My cell phone was back at the house on the microwave, an electronic device covered under the search warrant and not available to me when I trekked away from home.

My family. Were they looking for me? Were they so wrapped up in the sudden disruption of their lives by the actions of their husband and father that they had forgotten about me and my absence? I had no sense of whether I was missed or hated. Maybe I was missed because I was hated and Jackie wanted nothing more than to scream at my face and slug me.

I folded the knife and placed it in my pocket. I wasn't going to kill myself that day. I simply put the knife away.

I began thinking of options, given I was certain my family had by then disowned me and the police were out searching for me so they could arrest me, lock me up and throw away the key. I imagined what it would be like to be a homeless person on the streets of Vancouver or perhaps a bushman living out of a pine tree lean-to high in the mountains above Peachland.

It was ridiculous. I wasn't dressed for a walk in the woods a mile from my home. I certainly wasn't prepared for an extended stay in the wild. I could imagine trying to hitch a ride to Vancouver looking like I had rolled through a campfire and smelling as bad.

"Stupid, stupid, stupid," I said.

With grey clouds scattering sunlight overhead I had little concept of time. At some point, I noticed the light dwindling. I was surprised that nightfall was beginning. I couldn't have arrived creek side much later than 9:30 in the morning and already the day was turning to night. I had spent the entire day wallowing in my own misery and thinking about the past.

Having rained on and off all day and with little sunlight filtering down to the level of the creek, I got cold. I was cold, lonely, tired, hungry and miserable. I had no coat. I had nothing, save a pack of smokes, a lighter and the knife. I had nothing. That's the way I felt, that I had nothing. I had lost everything. My family, my life, my everything.

Today mom went to the store by herself.

Sometimes we go together. It's not queer for a boy my age to go to the grocery store with his mom. Sometimes I get a treat and that's cool. Sometimes I go by myself. I can carry a paper grocery bag in one arm and steer my bike with the other hand, so I'm good to go.

"David, I'm going to the store." That's what she said before she walked out the door.

It would have been silly for me to tell her that the second the door clicked shut a timer began running in my head. I never told her about the timer and I didn't tell her today.

Tick, tock, goes the timer.

I know how far the grocery store is from our house. Five blocks. I know almost exactly how long it takes to drive there. It's a small store, so it doesn't take long to walk down every aisle and pick up the few things needed.

We never have a lot in the cupboards or fridge and mom only ever buys one or two bags of groceries at a time.

There's time needed to go through the checkout, then it's out to the car and then the short drive home. I know how long it should take to buy groceries. The timer is meant to time how long it actually takes.

The house is quiet, save for the hum of the refrigerator and the sounds of a TV show.

Tick, tock.

I sit at the dining room table. I leaf through a hard cover book on astronomy. I like science and the book is one of many that mom and dad bought in a collection offered for sale on a TV commercial.

Tick, tock.

I flip the pages, look at the full colour pictures and read the captions underneath. The timer continues to run.

Tick, tock. It must be getting close to time for her to come back. It's been the right amount of time.

I step away from the table and go to the kitchen window. Outside a car slowly plies the gravel street in front of our house, kicking up soft puffs of dust. The driveway is empty.

Where is she? It's been the right amount of time and she should be home by now. Shouldn't she? How long has it been? I think it's been long enough. She should be home.

It starts in my belly, uneasiness I have not become accustomed to, even though I've felt it many times before. The stirring becomes queasiness as I crane my neck to peer as far down the road toward the direction of the grocery store as I can, looking for mom's car.

Tick, tock.

Really, it has to be time. She should be done by now. She should be pulling up any second. What's taking so long? Where is she? She probably stopped to talk to someone or maybe the store is busy today. Why today? It's Tuesday. It's never busy on Tuesday. Where is she? What could she be doing?

I walk from the kitchen window back to the book on the table and flip a few pages. I walk back to the kitchen window. As I peer outside, my right hand forms a fist and begins squeezing and releasing, squeezing and releasing. It is spring and cool outside and my breath leaves a haze on the window as I breathe heavily against the pane.

Something happened to her. I know something happened to her. She tripped walking to her car with a paper bag of groceries, her feet went out from under her and her legs landed on the paved parking lot, and a car ran over them. Oh shit. Oh God. Oh God, did that happen? It's so real. There it is, the car driving slow, the black rubber tires slowly rolling up and over mom's legs, the scream, the look of horror on mom's face, the sound of cracking bone. Is that what happened?

Both my hands pump in unison as the window becomes too fogged to look out. I walk fast through the dining room to the living room and flip open the big, heavy curtain to get a better view through the picture window. My breathing comes in gasps, my eyebrows scrunch down and I start to scratch one arm, hard.

Tick, tock.

She got into an accident. She was driving home and a car came around the corner and smashed into her. I see it. I see the car in slow motion driving through the intersection and there's mom's car driving perpendicular to the other car and there's mom sitting behind the wheel and she doesn't see the other car and there it is, the big crash, the front end of the other car slowly pushing into mom's door and there's mom flopping around like a rag doll. She's crumpled over in the front seat and there's blood and she's not moving. Is that an ambulance siren I hear?

I pace from the living room to the kitchen, peer out the window then run back to the living room, throwing the curtain open. With my hands and face pressed against the glass, I can see clear down to the curve in the road but there's no car, no mom. I'm no longer thinking in my head. I'm screaming.

Where is she? She should be here by now! Something is wrong! Something is wrong with my mom! Where is she? Could she have slipped on the parking lot and been run over? Did she have an accident? She hit a gravel truck. That's what it is. She hit a gravel truck and, oh no, I'm going to lose my mom. For sure, something happened. It's way past time. She should be home by now.

Tears well up in my eyes. My face feels like it's so hot it's on fire. My fists pump rhythmically as I stare out the picture window and fog the glass with my hot breath. Another car, this one faster, drives along the road, blotting out the view toward the grocery store with a cloud of dust. I'm going to throw up. I feel every part of my body, as if little pinpricks are touching every part of skin from my toes to my head.

Tick, tock.

I'm alone. I'm so alone. Where is she?

Suddenly out of the mist of street gravel dust, a red form emerges. It's red, it's a car, and it's... mom. My eyes roll up into my head and I let out a sigh as I mouth the words, "Oh thank God."

The red Ford Maverick pulls into our driveway and I see mom behind the wheel. Everything is okay. Everything except the gut-wrenching feeling I have throughout my whole body. I know it will take hours for the feeling to go away.

The temperature continued to drop, as did the sun. I had no clue what to do but I knew it wouldn't be a good idea to stay in my charcoal crypt overnight. I probably wouldn't make it, though that thought didn't particularly scare me.

I stood creek side and slowly raised my head, peering up the side of the gorge to where, near the top, the trail ran. I was surprised how far up the trail must be. Several hundred feet.

Slipping and sliding along, I began to ascend the slope toward the trail. The going was tough. That day's rain had made the ash covered ground even more slick than when I had traversed down slope. Several times, I took a step up only to slide down on loose gravel or slick grass.

By my recollection, it took 45 minutes for me to climb the slope, which included several breaks due to exhaustion. By the time I reached the trail I was sweating, cold, lonely, tired, hungry and miserable. Given the time of year and the lack of light around, I estimated it was 10 o'clock. I couldn't see the trail very well. There was little noise around me.

I could take the trail to the right, which wound its way up into the Trepanier Valley and eventually reached, well, nowhere. Alternatively, I could turn left and head back to Peachland.

I don't know why I chose the way I did. I walked slowly on the dark trail, not too worried about running into any hikers at that late hour. Somehow, I missed a fork in the trail and ended up veering right. I suddenly found myself at the end of a street in the Ponderosa neighbourhood.

My legs hurt from all the climbing and walking. I was not used to a lot of physical activity and the day's sullen adventure was far more than I had accomplished in a very long time. Streetlights lit the way as I sorely ambled down Sixth Avenue and then further down on Ponderosa Drive.

As I descended the mountainside, I kept an eye out for vehicles. I am well-known in Peachland and I did not want someone in a car seeing me and stopping to see if I needed help. I didn't want to talk to anyone. If I saw a car's headlights, I would jump over the concrete barrier on the side of the road and flatten myself to the ground until the car passed.

It took ages to walk the several hundred metres from Sixth Avenue down to the top of the Eagles View development. I stepped over a concrete barrier there and sat on the ground. Before me, past the development below, was Okanagan Lake. I could see all of downtown Peachland and, to the left a bit, the area of town where my house stood.

Resting on the ground and feeling numb in body and mind, I tried to figure out what I was doing at that place, at that time. Nothing made sense to me and I really had no idea where I was headed. As far as I knew, I had nowhere to go. I stared left and spied 13th street. My eyes followed the street until it intersected with Lake Avenue. There was the house on the corner. Beside it was our house. My eyes went wide. I could barely comprehend what I saw.

The back porch light on our house was on.

A worrywart, that's what I was at 12. I worried about everything, real and imagined. I worried about my grades at school, whether teachers liked me, if other kids liked me, if my notes and formulas were neat enough in my notebooks, you name it.

I didn't tell anyone about my worrying. If I got an award in school, an A on a test or was chosen to miss half a class to photocopy papers for a teacher in the office, the worrying seemed trivial. It all seemed like making a big deal over nothing. I didn't tell because the vast majority of times, when I did worry, everything turned out fine.

What I didn't know in those early days was that worrying was, really, the least of my worries. I had no clue what was going on and thought what I was going through was more or less what everyone went through. There was no indication to me that something more sinister than a healthy dose of worrying was at play. I was oblivious.

The signs were there, even early on. Easy for me to say now that I'm over-the-hill and headed down the other side. Not so easy for a preteen to figure out. On one hand, there was the anxiety. By 12, I was generally an anxious boy, far more wound up than my peers and easily excited to a higher state of the physical sensation of worry. I suffered frequent bouts of sweaty palms, a light-headed sensation, a creeping, under-the-skin feeling on the back of my head, headaches, nausea and a weird pins and needles feeling all over. When it got bad, I'd slide into a panic attack, with shortness of breath, a sense of impending dread, the feeling I was going to die and a pounding heart in my chest.

On the other hand, there were signs of something else going on, something more troubling yet easily confused with something else. I would get what someone might rightfully think, at first glance, was separation anxiety, but there was more to it than anxiety over being alone. There was the rhythmic opening and closing of my fists, the way I'd scratch my forearms from wrist to elbow, up and down and up again. There was pacing back and forth, a huge desire for the anxiety to go away and then there was the bad thing about being separated from a loved one. My mind didn't just run wild with speculation as to their demise. I actually saw them become disfigured or dead in my mind. I saw horrible, gruesome enactments of accidents in my head, as if I was standing right there watching them.

The separation anxiety didn't just happen when someone left me. It would start when I left others I cared about too. I could leave a friend's house after a visit and be instantly plunged into a state of high anxiety. I worried something bad was going to happen or was happening. I'd see something gruesome play out in my mind.

It's one thing to worry that someone you love has been involved in a car accident. It's another thing entirely to see the accident unfold, see and hear the crunching of metal on metal, see arms and legs flying all over, see a head smash into a windshield, see blood and brain matter splatter.

Two years before my junior high school got its first video tape player (it was the size of a large suitcase and played Beta tapes) I was watching horrific instances of maiming, brutality and death inside my head. It was very much like watching a videotape that happened to be playing in my mind.

Watching these mind-videos unfold always sent my anxiety level sky high. I'd cry out to myself in silence for the program to end, to be spared the horrific images flooding my brain. For hours after, I chastised myself for thinking such bad things and questioned myself as to why I came up with such twisted images.

I questioned my own sanity.

Jackie was a stickler for leaving the outside light on anytime it gets dark and someone was expected home. Surely, Jackie and Aaron were both inside the house, dealing somehow with the events of the day. That could only mean, would only mean, that Jackie was expecting someone to arrive that night. There was no other family in the area expected to show up that night. She was expecting me.

I stared for a long time at that light. It became a beacon of hope on a truly dismal day. The last thing I was thinking was that my family wanted me home. I had a hard time comprehending that after everything I put my family through they would still want me back.

I started walking. Every step down Ponderosa Drive was a step closer to home but also a step closer to reality. As the last vestiges of light left the sky above me, I concentrated only on putting one foot in front of another. My mind had long since shut down, unable to comprehend anything beyond the light that beckoned to me from the distance.

By the time I got to the bottom of Ponderosa Drive, where it meets Highway 97, it was pitch-black outside. It was just as well since I must have looked a fright, covered in ash and black sludge from my day near the creek.

I crossed the highway then walked the block to our street. I turned left and ended up in the exact place I had stood the previous morning prior to leaving to get a cup of coffee. I stood in the gravel parking area behind our back yard and the Oasis. There were no cop cars in sight.

I didn't know what to do. I stood there, looking at the fence around our yard. I didn't know if I should open the gate and walk in. Thoughts went through my head. Should I think of something to say? Should I have something to say before I open the back door? I froze.

As hard as it was for me to walk away again, I did exactly that. I slowly walked down the street, in the opposite direction I had come from. My mind simply would not work. I took a right, then another right onto Beach Avenue, arriving in front of our house but standing on the grassy lakeside area across the street. My heart jumped when I saw the front porch light on.

Sitting on the pebble beach across from my home, I stared out at the dark lake waters. Barely a ripple broke the light of the waning gibbous moon cast on the water. I half crawled to a wood lookout point that juts over the beach. I shut down. I was incapable of feeling the fear I knew must be just under the surface. I was incapable of feeling anything. I was tired, so tired. I slid my feet out from underneath me and lay on the beach. For the second time that day, I fell asleep, this time metres from my front door.

The highway is a long, unbroken strand of asphalt receding off into the distance. Fields of wheat bracket the road on both sides, only set off by the occasional side road or clump of poplar trees. We're on our way to another Al Anon meeting.

Dad was an alcoholic and when he quit drinking, a couple of years before I was born, he joined Alcoholics Anonymous. He became passionate about the 12 steps to recovery. Mom joined Al Anon, a group for those living with alcoholics.

Mom is the delegate from Alberta to the yearly Al Anon convention in New York City and many times, especially in summer, she drives from one town to another bringing the latest news to groups huddled in church basements. I'm only 12 so I have to go with her. It's boring.

Traffic is sparse on the highway. The odd family car whizzes by in the opposite direction. Sometimes we are stuck behind heavy transport trucks. We drive on. There's no air conditioning in the Maverick so our windows are down. It's hot and stuffy. I have on a T-shirt, a pair of tube socks pulled up to below my knees and a pair of white Adidas shorts. I'm sitting in the front passenger seat and I'm sweating.

I glance up from my Hardy Boy's adventure book and see off in the distance a vehicle heading toward us. The world slowly loses focus in the periphery as my attention falls solely on the vehicle. It gets bigger as it speeds toward us. Out of a mirage caused by sunlight reflecting off hot pavement, the blurry vehicle resolves into a truck. A big truck. A gravel truck.

From deep within my mind, an urge begins to surface. It's like a big hand inside me, pulling me to do a deed I don't want to do. The urge quickly gets stronger and stronger as the gravel truck in the opposing lane approaches us.

My left hand slides across the space between mom and me. It grabs the lower left segment of the steering wheel. I can see the driver of the gravel truck through the windshield as I jerk the wheel toward me, sending mom's car across the yellow line. I stare fixedly at the grill of the massive truck as the front end of mom's car meets it. The world goes black.

I'm frozen in place. I don't want mom to hear my breath so I silently pant as I stare out the windshield of our car at nothing but asphalt and wheat fields. The gravel truck is already a mile behind us, steadily increasing the distance between us. We're okay. Our car never left our lane.

Would I really have done it? Would I? Why did I see myself do it? I grabbed the wheel and I jerked the car over. Why would I do that? Am I bad? Am I a bad boy who wants to die and kill his mom? Why did I want to drive our car into the front of the truck? Why? Why does this keep happening? This is the third time today. Why?

I continue to breathe shallowly and return my gaze to the Hardy Boy's book on my lap. I don't feel much like reading but I don't want mom to think anything is wrong. What went through my mind will stay a secret, like all the other secrets.

I awoke as if from a dreamy fog. Disoriented, I looked around me. Gentle waves lapped at the shoreline. I was lying under the lookout point. The moon was up. Peachland was dark.

Sitting up, I fished my cigarettes from my pocket. I lit one as several cars cruised past on Beach Avenue behind me. The town was incredibly quiet. Finishing my smoke, I crawled out from under the lookout and stood on the beach. The front porch light remained on at my home. I began to walk.

I had no idea what time it was. Part of me thought it had only been a few hours since I left my house to get a coffee but the moon high in the night sky told a different story. I walked tentatively toward the front of our house. The blinds on the front picture window were half way down and it seemed like all was quiet inside. I peered through the window and suddenly I saw movement.

The front door flew open and Jackie barrelled out like a woman on a mission. I began walking away and put my hands on my head.

"I can't do this. I can't do this," I said.

"Yes you can. Get in the house," said Jackie as she took hold of me like a mother wrestling her child from danger.

"Get in the house," she repeated.

I surrendered. I let Jackie lead me inside the house. She guided me to the sofa that backed on the front window. I sat. I put my head in my hands. I was home.

Seventeen hours had passed since I walked away.

Chapter 3
Dirty Thoughts

Grand Centre in the 1970s was a dusty, mosquito-infested place in summer and a frozen wasteland in winter. It was the central hub between Cold Lake five miles to the north and the air force base two miles west. Cold Lake was the end of the highway, three hours northeast of Edmonton in Alberta. The town served the thousands of people who worked on the base and was the jumping off point to the oil fields north of Cold Lake where black, tarry bitumen was forced out of the earth with incredibly hot steam.

Our little house was tucked in behind one of the service roads running parallel to the highway on a quiet, gravel road. A block and a bit from home was the highway and across it and up the hill a ways was Grand Centre Junior High School.

Junior high was for me a time of excelling in academics,

the best friendships I ever had and the beginning of terrible thoughts that invaded my world.

It was a bitch being 12-years-old and having the picture of my only living parent mauled to death in a brutal car accident burned into my head. It wasn't just a picture. It was more like a video of the act, a desperately creepy short movie in my brain that I couldn't turn off. There was only one channel in my mind and it was a full blast, colour, live performance of something hideous that often involved someone I loved.

There's no telling when the video would appear. At first, it was times when I was stressed out, anxiety-ridden. If mom left me at home and didn't come back when I thought she should, a mind-video would play out. Maybe I'd get to thinking about my oldest sister who was teaching in a small town in southern Alberta. I'd get to missing her and if I thought about it too much, my thoughts turned to my sister and became horrific and painful. Loved ones became involved in bizarre and scary scenes inside my head.

The thoughts changed over time. No longer did I have to think of a family member or even a friend to bring on the nasty mind-video thoughts. I'd be 12 or 13 and walking down the street and suddenly, out-of-the-blue, with no effort on my part, I'd see one of my brothers stabbed in the back with a nine-inch blade. Or I'd see Brent hit a rock on his bike. He'd fly over the handlebars and then his face would hit the gravel road and be shredded to bits as he ground to a halt.

It hurt badly. There were times I would grab my head and try to pull the thoughts out of my mind. Other times I'd smash the heels of my hands on my forehead.

"Go away. Please, please go away," I'd say to myself.

The thoughts terrified me. Not only were the mind-videos gruesome to watch, but they were so incredibly real. Watching a horrific scene play out in the theatre of my mind was as real as if it was happening in front of me. There was no difference between witnessing a death in real life and watching it unfold inside my head.

My breathing would change. I'd grit my teeth. I'd sweat. The sweat would bring with it a flush of heat, then a shiver from the icy depths of hell. My eyes would frantically dart around. I'd look to see if anyone could notice something wrong with me and figure out I was having an episode or, worse, could peer into my mind and see what I had seen.

It was always bad. It didn't matter how many times I had seen a grotesque mind-video play out in my mind. Every time it happened, it was fresh, new, frightening and real.

I was petrified that someone would find out. Often, I felt that people around me could sense my mind was dreaming up grotesque visions. The last thing I wanted was for my mom or siblings or a teacher at school to stare at me with knowing eyes, recognizing that I was sick and twisted.

That was junior high. That and a whole lot more.

I'd be sitting in class. It could be Grade 7, 8 or 9. I'd be sitting there and the teacher would be droning on. I would be taking notes like a good pupil, but not a good pupil paying full attention. As much as I tried to be attentive in class, my attention would be snatched away from me by some thought ramming its way into my consciousness.

Every one of these thoughts demanded attention. I would cave and think about the thought and by thinking about the thought I wasn't thinking about what the teacher was saying or trying to teach me and I'd lose time. I'd lose time a lot.

I would lose segments of every class. I swear that's why, when I took year end exams, I'd stare at the exam papers and get frustrated because I was sure, absolutely sure, we never took that stuff in class. Either we didn't take certain stuff in class or I had blocked out some of the subject matter.

The thoughts that would show up out of nowhere were really bad. I didn't want them. I wanted them to go away. I didn't know if everyone else around me was also having scary, anxiety provoking thoughts but I sure didn't like the ones I was getting.

One particular thought that showed up often in class really scared the pants off me. I hated when it showed up and it always seemed to show up at the worst possible time.

Mr. Brown stands at the front of the class. He's talking about geography and how the map of the world has changed countless times over the centuries. A large map is rolled down from above the blackboard. He has a piece of chalk in his right hand, which he uses to emphasize certain points he's making by poking it in the air. His left hand resides in the pocket of his corduroy sports coat.

The class is quiet. Some of my fellow students take notes. Most look bored and ready for lunch.

Suddenly I stand up. I face Mr. Brown. I take a deep breath in then yell.

Fuckin' son-of-a-bitch you fucking prick you fucking cocksucking son-of-a-bitch who do you think you are you fucking bastard you fucking prick you cocksucker, motherfucker, fuck, fuck it, fuck.

I'm sweating. My breath comes in wheezes and huffs.

My eyes are wide as I take in the scene around me. I'm still sitting. Mr. Brown drones on. The kid beside me has glazed over eyes.

It never happened.

It felt so real. It always feels real. I slowly turn my head around to see if anyone notices there's something wrong.

"Eyes front, David," says Mr. Brown. I look straight ahead and breathe with a rasp.

I hate this so bad. I hate it so much, it happens so much, and I really, really wish it would go away. I was sitting at my desk and then I was standing up and swearing my head off. I was swearing all those bad words and yelling them, yelling them out and oh shit why does this keep happening? Does it mean I'm going to do it? I've never actually done it but maybe next time I'll do it, I'll do it for sure or maybe I won't but it feels like I'm so going to do it. I don't want to do it. I don't want to swear my head off. Why do I think this? Why does this go through my head and why do I see myself swearing?

Sometimes it happens when I'm sitting there, minding my own business. Other times it happens when I'm called on to answer a question or if I have to go to the front of the class to give a report. It usually happens when I'm standing there at the blackboard, in front of everyone, like a deer in the headlights.

Every time it happens, I see myself standing up and yelling every bad word I ever learned at everyone in the room. I can almost hear myself say the words and I definitely think the words, as they seem to puke out of my mouth.

My mind gets stuffy full of other thoughts when an episode is over. It's like thoughts on top of thoughts.

Did I just swear like that and scream? No one said anything. Maybe I didn't do it. But it feels so real. It felt like I actually did it. What if I did it? No the teacher would have grabbed me and hauled me out in the hall. I didn't do it. But I could have, right? It's happened before and I never actually did it but this time felt so real. Does anyone know? Did the teacher see something in my face so that he knows I was thinking something really bad? I was facing the teacher when I said it or thought I said it so did he see me? Did he maybe see my mouth move a bit? I feel sick. I could have done it. I'm scared. What if next time whatever stops me from doing it doesn't work and I actually do it and the teacher and all the other students hear me scream and yell and swear all those bad words? What if? What if I can't stop it? What if it really happens? Why does this keep happening? I have to tell someone. No, they'll think I'm crazy.

So many strange thoughts and behaviours began in junior high school. It was like someone upended a box of scary thoughts into my head, all jumbled around, and they randomly showed up when I least expected them.

I became obsessed with the order of things. Not so much organizing pencils in a pencil case or making sure books on a shelf were in alphabetical order, because I didn't do that sort of thing when I was young. No, the order I became fixated on was that of what came first, the chicken or the egg.

I'd be riding my bike down the road and I'd see a car heading toward me in the opposite lane. I'd also spy a yield sign on my side of the road. The thought would pop into my head that I had to pass the yield sign before the car passed me. The race would be on. I would pump the pedals hard to ensure I got to the yield sign on time.

In our little kitchen in our little house, I'd be washing dishes in the sink and mom would pull up in her car outside. A thought would suddenly arise that I had to finish the two plates in the sink before mom walked in the door. The race would be on again, me frantically washing and rinsing plates in a desperate struggle to finish before my mom walked in the door.

There was no rhyme or reason for the A before B thoughts. They could pop up at any time and involve almost anything, always involving two opposing situations, one of which had to be done or completed before the other. I can't really say why I had to do A before B, but I guess it was a sense that something bad would happen if it didn't end up that way.

There were even times when the goal was clearly out of reach, like the car was far too close and therefore I could not get to the yield sign on time. Then a different thought would pop into my head. Then I'd have to pedal nine times before the car passed me. It was like a way out of the impossibility of getting to the yield sign on time by having a new, secondary way of putting A before B.

I'd end up having these sorts of mental races all throughout a day. Time was always my enemy. The thought might show up that I had to finish a certain number of questions at the end of Chapter 3 in my math book before the clock hit the bottom of the hour. I might have to get my books out of my locker before a certain teacher walked by me. There were times I had to finish eating, either a mouthful, all of something on my plate, or my whole meal, by the time some innocuous thing happened.

I didn't think much about the consequences of not doing A before B. I think it would have been too terrible to contemplate and, besides, I never had the time to sit down and analyze the situation. I had to get my butt in gear and get A done before B came along, or else.

I open the front door of the school and walk out into the sunshine. It's April and Grade 8 will soon be ending. Walking along the dusty roadway, I kick the odd rock down the hill toward the highway. I get to the bottom of the hill and take the sidewalk across the highway. I walk through the front door of the corner store. I have $3 in my pocket and I'm on a mission.

A creepy feeling envelops me as I check out the bags of chips on a rack. The owner's wife is behind the counter to ring through purchases while the owner keeps one eye on me from the back of the store. I'm a teenager and that means the level on the owner's trust-o-meter is pretty low.

I grab a bag of salt and vinegar chips and head to the chocolate bar rack. There's a lot to choose from and I take my time. My hand darts out to grab a bar, and then is withdrawn with indecision. After several fitful starts, I grab a Caravan, my favourite bar, and set it along with the chips on the counter.

The owner's wife presses a button on the cash register. Suddenly a thought coalesces in my head.

There's a chocolate bar in my jacket pocket. I stole a chocolate bar.

Instantly I break out in a cold sweat. Imperceptibly, I begin to shake.

There's a chocolate bar in my pocket. I stole the bar and I'm going to be caught.

I swallow hard and try not to look guilty. The owner's wife keeps pressing buttons on the cash register. I very, very slowly turn my head to the left to look down the aisle. There's the owner, staring back at me.

Does he know I stole the chocolate bar? Did he see me put in my pocket? What's he going to do? Is he going to run up, grab me, and accuse me of stealing? Will he call my mom? What will my mom say when she finds out I stole a chocolate bar?

I slip my left hand into a jacket pocket and feel around. All that's in there is a Pink Pearl eraser. I shuffle my feet a bit. I look around slowly, hoping I don't look guilty. I slip my right hand into my other jacket pocket and feel around. There's nothing there but the silky pocket lining. My breath comes out as a whisper but it seems louder than a freight train. I continue to sweat and don't dare draw attention to myself by looking back at the owner at the back of the store.

I stole a chocolate bar and it's in my pocket.

Oh, crap why did I steal a chocolate bar? I don't remember taking one and putting it in my pocket but I have a bar in my pocket. Oh, crap. What am I going to do? I could put it back. Yeah. I could put it back and it will all be all right but I'd have to take it out of my pocket and the owner will see. He's looking right at me and he'll see me pull it out of my pocket and I'll get caught. I shouldn't do anything. I should leave the chocolate bar in my pocket and try to leave. No, I'll be caught. Crap. What should I do?

"That's $1.19 please," the owner's wife says from behind the counter.

I slip both hands into my back pockets. Empty. I quickly slip both hands into my front pockets and feel only the crumpled up dollar bills in one pocket. I pull them out, smooth out two on the counter and slide them over.

My change comes back and I slip it into my pocket. I hurriedly grab the chocolate bar and the chips and walk out of the store. I'm freaking out and I want to get away from the store as fast as I can. I walk around the corner and down the street. About a block away, I stop and let out a sigh.

It felt so real. It felt so real I could have sworn it was real. It was as real as it is that I'm standing on a sidewalk half a block from my house. It was as real as my jacket, my jeans, me. It felt so real. Again.

There were times in junior high that it felt like every day there was a new type of weird and disturbing thought entering my head. Sometimes I would sit and stare at my classmates, looking at them intently, wondering if they too had thoughts in their heads that made them shake with fear.

Do they try to drive cars into oncoming traffic? Do they freak out when their mom, dad, sister, or brother leaves their house and fails to come back on time? What if they leave their best friend's house? Do they stop a few hundred yards away and wonder if something bad is happening at the house they left? If they go to a store and they get to the checkout counter do they suddenly get the feeling like they've stolen something? Do they have to do one thing before they have to do another? Have they ever sat in class and thought about jumping up and swearing every dirty swear word at the top of their lungs?

If they did think such things then I guessed I wouldn't be so alone. If they didn't have thoughts like that going through their heads then I was not only alone but absolutely nuts.

On one hand, I was popular in school, with teachers and students alike. I got good grades, got invited to parties, had about the same number of friends as anyone else and even got elected as valedictorian of my Grade 9 class. On the other hand, I was so alone. I couldn't talk to anyone about the thoughts. They were too scary, too awful, even disgusting and gruesome.

I couldn't know for sure but I was fairly sure the other kids in my school weren't having thoughts as I was. For sure, no one else ever talked about it. Since they didn't talk about it, neither did I. I kept it a secret.

If I had blurt out to someone that I was having alarming thoughts I was afraid, really afraid, that I'd be taken away and put into some kind of hospital somewhere. I thought often of that, of being arrested by the police or having some kind of white van pull up to the house and two big brutes step out to fetch me and take me off to some nasty place where sick kids with sick thoughts go.

As time went on, the thoughts became more complex and more frequent. It started out slow for sure, but by the time I stepped out of junior high for the last time in the summer of 1978, the thoughts were firing on all cylinders. The weird thoughts I had in Grade 6 paled in comparison to the hideous thoughts I had by the end of Grade 9. Over time, not only did the thoughts come more frequently, but also they became more disturbing.

Many was the night that I would seek refuge at home as best as I could. One of my favourite places was on the living room rug, lying on my side with my head propped up by one hand, watching TV. It was a position guaranteed to cause a sore arm or a crick in the neck, but it afforded me the ability to watch the TV without having to look at anybody else in the room. I could be alone among family and alone with my thoughts.

My bedroom was the best place for solace. Many days I lay on my bed alone, thinking about the thoughts and how they affected me. I thought about thinking about the thoughts.

One of the more disturbing thoughts that started entering my mind in junior high was the question of my sexuality.

Junior high was a terribly complex time for everyone. Sexuality burgeoned, things started growing. Hair starts sprouting up in places where it had never been before. Everybody, pretty much, starts to get interested in sex – even just the concept of sex. I had the required amount of becoming-a-teenager angst and more than enough other angst to open up an angst store.

Hoping beyond hope, all I really wanted was to grow up the right way. I hoped that everything was progressing along normally, that my body was changing the way it should. I wanted very much for girls to show an interest in me. I sure was interested in them and in the way their bodies changed as junior high progressed.

I was quite shy around girls. I got along with them all right. I could talk to them and stand next to them and even joke around. However, I was shy in the asking-a-girl-out department, something that was rife in our school. It seemed like everybody was going out with someone, even if the pairings seemed to change more often than I changed my socks.

This shyness led to feeling less than stellar in the sexuality department. I didn't know if I had what it took to get a girlfriend and do all the things that girlfriends and boyfriends are supposed to do with each other. It didn't help that I was getting thoughts that made me question my sexuality.

Like most of my other disturbing thoughts, these thoughts could come at any time. They most often came when I was around friends and other students at school. For the most part the thoughts came in the form of a question like, *Am I a faggot?*

Being called a dweeb was bad enough but the worst thing any boy could be called in junior high was a faggot. No one used the term gay or homosexual. We were cruel in the late 1970s. It was faggot. A boy that was into boys was a faggot. A boy who didn't seem like he was all boy was a faggot.

It's not like I sat around thinking whether I was into girls or not. I liked girls just fine. The thoughts would show up in my head. I didn't have to say anything or do anything to make them appear.

The thoughts would morph too. They would go from the question, *Am I a faggot,* to a statement like, *I think he's good-looking. I think he's cute.* I could glance at another boy in my school and suddenly it was as if I had a thought machine inside my head and it would generate a random thought along the lines of whether I was into boys or not.

I didn't want to be a faggot. Oh, hell no I didn't want to be a faggot. I knew all the jokes that kids my age cracked. If you didn't have a girlfriend or weren't actively being overly friendly with girls, you could easily be labelled a faggot and that was a label that no junior high kid wanted.

Yet there I was, sitting in class in junior high school, or riding my bike down the street, or sitting at home on my bed reading a book, or some such thing, and a thought like, *Am I a faggot?* would hammer its way into my mind and I'd freak out.

When a thought like that would enter my head, the first thing I do is freeze. It was like a shock to my system. Brain overload. Then I'd try my damndest to push the thought out of my head. Force it out; push it away like an annoying classmate who bugged me about my haircut. Then I'd have conversations with myself, inside my head.

Am I a faggot? Am I attracted to that boy? Maybe I am a faggot because I'm looking at him and he has a nice face and a skinny body and... No! No! I don't want to be a faggot. I'm not a faggot. I like girls! No, I like boys. I know I'm a faggot and into boys. No! I don't want to be. I want to have a girlfriend like everyone else. I don't want to be like this! I want to kiss him. I want to hold him and touch him. I don't want this! Please go away. I didn't ask you to come inside my head and make me think this way. Go away! I'm a faggot and everyone knows I'm a faggot. No they don't. No they don't. I'm not a faggot and not everyone thinks that. I don't have a girlfriend and that means I'm a faggot. I like that boy, I can tell. No I don't!

It didn't help that in junior high I had the ability to pop a boner at the suggestion of a stiff wind, let alone for any sexual reason. The damn thing had a mind of its own and would start rising for no reason whatsoever. It made it very bad when I started to get an erection or feel a twinge down below when the question of my sexuality was raised inside my head.

I feel that. I feel that down in my crotch. I'm getting excited by that boy. I looked at that boy, something moved down there, and that means I want that boy. That means I'm a faggot. Accept the truth. I saw that boy and I felt something down there and that means I like boys and that means I'm a faggot. Only boys who get excited about other boys are faggots and that means I am one. I have to be one because I felt it.

It made it worse that I would get the same kind of physical sensations when I looked at a cute girl. I believed I was straight. I wanted to be straight. I got twinges in my groin if I saw a cute girl in tight jeans and a tight top. To me that meant the physical feeling was confirmation of being straight. But then I would get exactly the same sensations when I looked at a boy and in my mind that meant I really was interested in him. I thought that meant I was into boys.

It was a confusing time beyond reason. I couldn't wrap my head around the prospect of liking boys and girls at the same time. Furthermore, I personally liked girls in a gee-I-want-to-be-your-boyfriend kind of way. I didn't like boys in that way. I would think about girls. I wanted to think about girls. I thrived on thinking about girls. Nevertheless, the thoughts about boys kept showing up in my head and I didn't want to think about boys.

It didn't seem to matter how hard I tried to push the thoughts away, I kept having thoughts that made me question whether I was gay or not.

Compounding the problem I had with having nasty thoughts of a sexual nature was what I can only describe now as a somewhat warped or twisted sex education.

I think it was Thursday. Something tells me that the day the new magazines came in was Thursday.

Grand Centre was a small town by every description. Only 3,500 people called it home, but it did have two drugstores. One of those stores, the one on the main street and across the street from the grocery store, had a big garbage bin out back.

Once a week, sure as clockwork, the new magazines came in to that drugstore. When a new issue of a magazine came in, one of the clerks took the old issue off the stand and then tore the cover off. The cover went back to the distributor for credit, while the remainder of the magazine was summarily chucked out.

There were boxes and boxes of old magazines, sans covers, thrown into that garbage bin every week.

Quite a few boys in town knew what day magazine day is. We also knew that intermingled in the Time, National Geographic and Vogue coverless magazines was a good smattering of magazines of a much more sophisticated nature. Nudie magazines.

The drugstore was about the only place in town where one could purchase a magazine featuring photos of naked women, all tucked away on the top shelf of a high rack, lest little hands grab a hold when they had no business doing so.

Snagging a nudie or two meant waiting until the drugstore closed and the staff cars pulled out of the lot, and then sneaking over the side of the garbage bin, wading through the pile of cardboard and finding the right box of that day's castoffs. If you were late because you had to do dishes at home or some such thing, well you were out of luck. The nudies were gold and there were some serious prospecting teenagers in Grand Centre. Me included.

Sometimes I went to the drugstore with a friend. We'd snag a few magazines then take off to somewhere secluded to flip through the pages. Usually we were too embarrassed to talk to each other while looking.

I didn't have a dad to give me 'the talk'. Mom's version of educating me about the birds and bees was leaving a book on my usual TV chair that talked about masturbation as a sure fire way of growing hair on your palms. We definitely never talked about sex in our house. It was a private thing that was never to be mentioned in front of other people.

Sex education for me at the age of 13 or 14 came from a cardboard box of castoffs at the drugstore. The only formal sex education I received was in Grade 9. A public health nurse came to our homeroom. Over the course of one hour, the nurse instructed us what to expect as far as body changes (that had mostly already occurred) and how to put a condom onto a banana.

Mostly the students around me snickered and giggled nervously. I didn't learn anything I hadn't figured out already.

That's what sex education was like in northern Alberta in the 1970s. Part of me has always thought since I didn't get any kind of sex education at home and had to rely on the fanciful stories of buddies and the garbage from the local pharmacy that was at least one reason why I ended up so screwed up.

Somehow, I managed to figure out where all the parts were and how they were supposed to work. But the knowledge gained from a garbage bin and that one-hour talk in Grade 9 by the public health nurse wasn't enough to keep my head straight when it came to sex.

As junior high progressed, my thoughts started to become more and more bizarre and frightening when it came to the taboo subject of sex.

By the time I finished Grade 9 my mind was royally screwed. I had some bizarre thoughts running through my head. I couldn't seem to control them. Nothing I did seemed to matter or seemed to make the thoughts go away. They came relentlessly, some days focussing on one type and other days being a mish-mash of every kind of bad thought all together.

On many days, my thinking would be a menagerie of rammed together thoughts I didn't want. I so didn't want the thoughts, the way they would seep into my consciousness and steal otherwise fun moments.

Sometimes I wanted nothing more than to run away. I might be sitting there eating my lunch at school and thoughts would be popping off like popcorn in a hot skillet. A friend would be beside me talking about this or that and all I wanted to do was run away to a dark place where I could scream.

The thoughts disturbed me beyond words. I didn't ask them to be there. They just showed up. They started to show up so frequently that I knew they were coming and I'd be anxiously waiting for them to appear.

It was like being on a high level of alert all the time, fearful of having my brain assaulted again. Sure enough, it would be. Then my anxiety would go sky high because whatever the thought was it was never good; the thoughts were always bad and they made me sad.

As much as having thoughts about being gay or standing

up in class and swearing my head off rocked me from the inside, one type of thought that appeared in junior high was far more terrible and it made me so sad there were days I wanted to die. They made me feel like the worst kind of kid possible. Who but a sick deviant would think about hurting people until they bled or worse? Who but an insane person would think about killing their friends and family members?

Chapter 4
Dark Days

Sitting on the sofa at four o'clock in the morning, my mind refused to work. I was so overcome by emotion I had no emotion to express. I was home but I was lost. My mind shut down.

The police had long ago left, taking my laptop computer and leaving Jackie and my son Aaron to deal with the mess of the day and my absence. What they went through I could not imagine or comprehend.

Jackie woke Aaron up. He came down the stairs and gave me a big hug.

"I don't care what you did. I love you, dad," he said.

As I sat on the couch with my head in my hands, Jackie told me some of what went on that day with the police and the investigation but it wasn't sticking in my head. I couldn't focus on her words or appreciate their significance. I felt my life was over.

I was exhausted. Although I slept twice during my 17-hour truancy from life, I could barely keep my eyes open. I wanted to shut them. Shut out the world. I had returned to my family and to the shattered thing that was my life.

Jackie said the police had been out looking for me the afternoon before. She got a list of recent transactions on our bank account and knew I had gone to the convenience store.

"What did you buy at the dollar store?" she asked. I reached into my pocket and pulled out the knife. I handed it over to her.

My clothes stunk of burnt, wet forest. A layer of black grunge stuck to my jeans and shoes. Somehow, I made it up the stairs to the shower. I remember using a scrub brush on my feet. Soon after, I crawled into bed and mercifully fell into a deep sleep.

The day the police arrived unceremoniously at my house I was 49-years-old. I came to think of it as the Day from Hell. One day before, Jackie celebrated her 48th birthday. One month prior, we had celebrated our 25th wedding anniversary. We were the proud parents of two adult boys, Aaron, living with us, and his older brother Garrett, who lived at my sister Barb's home in Lethbridge, Alberta.

After spending eight years as the reporter for the town's only newspaper, I struck out on my own with an online newspaper. Although it did gain quite a few followers, it never really took off and it was in danger of collapsing under the weight of too much work and not enough income.

To say I was well-known in town would be an

understatement. Though not everyone in Peachland followed my news website, for eight years I was the person who reported on the goings on in town. I wrote every article and penned a weekly editorial that often got me in trouble with someone. I was well-known, recognizable and now very much in trouble.

I awoke sometime in the morning and, coffee in hand, went out to sit in the Oasis. The world seemed a whole lot darker than it had the morning before and I felt like I was living in a fog. It was a Friday.

My sister Barb was the oldest of our clan and the one who drops everything and runs to help when one of her brothers or sisters was in trouble. It was a foregone conclusion that she would hop on a plane in Lethbridge and take the two-hour flight to the Okanagan Valley to be with Jackie and me.

Barb arrived shortly after I awoke and, together with Jackie, sat with me in the back yard.

By the story Jackie told of her interaction with the police the day before, Barb got the gist of what had been going on. Clearly, I would have to provide some detail but there were no surprises anymore for my wife or for Barb.

Jackie told me that the police had kept her and Aaron outside for hours as they rifled through everything in our house. An undercover police officer chatted with someone on the Internet at the IP address associated with our house and that the conversations had involved children and sex.

The police asked Jackie questions. They wanted to know if I travelled a lot for business and what types of books I liked to read. Jackie told the police she didn't want to answer the questions. Her concern at the time was finding me. Questions could wait.

I found out that, at one point, Aaron could not sit at home waiting for me to return. He left to search for me. He ended up behind the elementary school, at the start of the Trepanier Gorge, yelling my name, pleading for me to come home. I never did hear Aaron from my hiding place near the creek, even though he had figured out where I was.

Believing that I might be a danger to myself, a number of police cars descended on Peachland. The officers went from business to business, asking employees if they had seen me that day. That realization made me cringe. It meant that some people in town, though perhaps oblivious to the reason behind it, knew something was wrong with me.

Little of what Jackie said to me that morning pierced the emotionless shell around me. One thing that did crack the shell was how, even after having her life tumbled upside down, she still loved me. In fact, I heard about love from both my sons and Barb that day and it did have an effect on me. Frankly, it was hard for me to figure out how anybody could love me after what I had done. However, there was a tiny glimmer of hope in the words. I said little sitting in the Oasis.

Jackie asked me why I took off. I mumbled something about being freaked out and wanting to get away and maybe end my life. She asked why I came back and I said I didn't know but I told her I saw the back porch light on from high up the mountainside.

I told Jackie and Barb how I went to the coffee shop, walked away and found myself on the trail high above the creek. How I chose a place to go down that made me slip and slide. How I ended up near the creek and crawled inside the burned out log. How I tripped on a log in the forest and scraped my shin enough for it to bleed. How coming back out I had to slip and slide my way up the canyon slope until I again reached the trail.

"Maybe you went to punish yourself," Barb suggested.

So ashamed of what I put my family through in the past 24 hours, I could not look Jackie and Barb in the eye. I kept my eyes down, staring off into space. It felt like I was wrapped in a cocoon that dulled my senses and wouldn't allow me to think straight.

"You need help," said Barb. She suggested that I was in crisis and that I needed to seek help, now. She then said I must go to see my doctor as a first step.

I was beyond the ability to think for myself or argue. All I could think was that my life was over and it didn't really matter what I did or said. In fact, I was so emotionally and mentally drained that for the first time since I was 11, the thoughts were silent.

Somehow I could drive. Barb sat in the front passenger seat as I drove the 10 minutes to my doctor's office. We drove along the highway and up Drought Hill, with the expansive blue waters of Okanagan Lake laid out to our right. Jackie stayed home. She was emotionally and mentally exhausted and needed some time alone.

Sitting in the waiting room at the doctor's office with Barb, I tried to get my brain to figure out how I was going to broach the subject of my current predicament with my doctor. I had been going to the same doctor for a number of years but we didn't really know each other. I wondered if that was a good thing.

Barb came with me as the receptionist led the way to a room at the back of the building. The wait was mercilessly short. I was beginning to panic again. The doctor came in and asked what he could do for me. I blurted it out. "The police came to my place yesterday for a child pornography investigation and I took off and was thinking about suicide."

The doctor listened then stood up and said he'd be right back. I had no clue what was going on or what he would do. For all I knew the paddy wagon would show up and I'd be carted off to some hospital somewhere.

Returning a few minutes later, the doctor produced a piece of paper with an address in Kelowna on it. "You have an appointment with Kelowna Mental Health. They're expecting you now."

Barb and I were off again. This time we drove the 15 minutes to Kelowna. I didn't know what Kelowna Mental Health was. It didn't matter. I was on autopilot. I knew the roads well enough and I just drove.

The actual name of the place we went to was Kelowna Mental Health and Substance Use. We arrived mid-afternoon and were confronted with a waiting room full of people.

I did not know what went on in that building. I didn't know who I was going to talk to, what we would talk about or where it would lead. I suspected whomever I met would be very interested in the fact that I took off for 17 hours and bought a knife. Part of me believed I might be told to get my butt to the hospital for an immediate admission.

I was given a questionnaire to fill out with all the obligatory questions like age, weight and a list of medications being taken. As I filled out the form, I started repeating syllables quietly to myself.

It's something I've done for as long as I can remember and only happens when I'm profoundly stressed. I repeat the ending syllables of some words. Usually those words end in 'ing'. I didn't know why I did it, but I either did it in my head or softly, out loud. I had to repeat 'ing' words until they sounded right. I could mindlessly do this for quite some time without really realizing I was even doing it.

Soon enough I was ushered into a quiet office by an intake worker. Barb stayed in the waiting room. I was numb. I quietly explained what had happened to me over the past 30 hours. With little emotion in my voice, I recapped the arrival of the police, why they were at my house, my walk out into the woods, the knife, my missing for 17 hours and my return home.

Many very careful questions were asked. The intake worker was trying to figure out if I was still a danger to myself and if something needed to be done about that. I knew neither Jackie nor Barb would leave me alone for a minute over the weekend. I told the intake worker I had the support of my family (though I didn't really understand why).

The intake worker was understanding and compassionate. Whatever I said to him didn't faze him in the least. I expected him to cluck his tongue and shake his head. All he seemed to care about was me. It was strange. I thought of myself as a very bad person, yet here was this trained professional showing me compassion and care.

I guess I answered his questions the right way. I wasn't loaded up in a van for a trip to the psych ward. Instead, I got a card with a phone number on it for the crisis prevention hotline. I also got an appointment with a crisis counsellor a few days in the future.

I drove home to an uncertain future.

The weekend I spent at home. I couldn't bear the thought of being out in the public, even if no one had a clue what had transpired at my house. I wouldn't know how to act in front of people. I wouldn't know what to say if the occasion called on me to say anything. I wanted to hide at home, even if doing so meant I would have to face my wife of 25 years and her questioning.

How do you tell your wife, your best friend, your life mate of over 25 years that you're a disgusting bastard who thinks wicked things? I didn't know. I couldn't figure out the right words to say.

I told Jackie that I was chatting on the Internet and that the conversations happened in a God-awful place involving a subject matter that was disgusting, vile and dangerous. The subject was, in fact, so vile that it brought the police to my house.

I was evil. Nobody chats about the things I chatted about without being twisted. Of that I was sure. I had bad thoughts. I had them for a very long time. There were levels of thoughts I had, from slightly disturbing to despicable. What I chatted about on the Internet was the lowest level of thoughts. They were the ones that caused me the most grief.

The police, it turned out, were eager to have a talk with me. Had I stayed at home the day they rifled through my house, they would have wanted to take Jackie, Aaron and I to the police station for separate interviews. They left our house without having a proper interview with anyone. The cops told Jackie that, once I returned home, I should call them to set up an interview time.

The Monday after the Day from Hell, I called the lead investigator from the Integrated Child Exploitation unit of the RCMP. We set up an interview at the Kelowna detachment for that Wednesday. It was a chance for me to tell my side of the story.

That sounded good. I should have a chance to tell my side of the story, even though my side sounded screwed up even to me. However, something didn't sit well over the whole thing and after a talk with Jackie, I decided to do something I had never had occasion to do in my life. I called a lawyer after a quick Google search.

I gave the lawyer a brief synopsis of what had transpired the previous Thursday. He told me that, under no circumstances, should I grant an interview to the police. He explained that the police were only interested in gaining evidence against me, not in determining guilt or innocence.

The police would prepare a report for the Crown prosecutor, who would decide if there was enough evidence to lay charges. The worst thing I could do was grant an interview.

I called the police back and declined an interview. The officer sounded almost sad on the phone but I felt that granting an interview was definitely the wrong thing to do. Why give the police more ammunition to use against me?

The one bad thing about not talking to the police was that I got no information from them. I had no idea what would happen next or how long it would take me to find out.

My fate was unknown.

<> <> <>

Driving to Kelowna for my first counselling session was not easy. The thought of having to tell another human being what I had done and the involvement of the police and the words 'child pornography' filled me with dread. I had already told my doctor and the intake worker and discussed it at length with Jackie and Barb. Now I would have to do it again.

Pulling into a parking space, I looked at the Interior Health Authority building. It's a large building. The main floor is taken up with various clinics, administration and other offices. The entire second floor was dedicated to mental health. It's a lot of space. Apparently, Kelowna was busy when it came to mental health.

I stepped out of the car and walked over to the ticket dispenser. I dropped a few coins in the slot, grabbed the printed ticket and went back to the car. I set the ticket on the dashboard, closed the door, pressed the lock button on my key fob and started walking toward the entrance door.

Did I lock the car?

I fished the key fob out of my pants pocket and pressed the lock button. I could hear the horn bleat. I started walking toward the front door.

Am I sure I locked the car?

I sighed in frustration. This thought was something new. I pressed the button again and walked through the front door. As I started up the stairs to the second floor, the thought came back.

Did I lock the car?

I didn't like the waiting room. It could hold about 25 people or so and many of them looked, well, weird. In the corner, a guy slowly rocked back and forth to a tune no one else could hear. Beside him, a guy kept tapping his fingers on his knee, which was going up and down to a different beat. The floor of the waiting room was mostly white but it had a red stripe down the room lengthwise. A guy walked on that red stripe, back and forth, back and forth. I waited.

Who knew why these people were in the same waiting room as me. This was Kelowna Mental Health and Substance Use, so there could be psychotics, schizophrenics, drug users and drug abusers in the waiting room.

I couldn't help but notice that here I was, a middle-aged, ordinary looking man sitting among mentally ill people, many of whom likely had a severe addiction. Part of me wanted to scream at the thought I was in the same place as these people. Part of me had to admit I fit right in. I was, after all, a man who was caught chatting on the Internet about unsavory subjects.

My therapist was an urgent response clinician with Kelowna Mental Health. He was one of a bunch of people who dealt with mental health and substance abuse problems at the office but he only dealt with people in crisis. I fit the bill.

I swallowed what little pride I had left and explained to him how I ended up in his office on a sunny summer day. It was July in the Okanagan Valley and that meant heat outside. In his office, I was cold and withdrawn, feeling isolated and trapped.

We talked about my crisis. My therapist was frank. I could be in for the long haul when it came to my legal problems. He said he dealt with people who had spent years in the court system before their cases were finally resolved. I couldn't know how prophetic his words ended up being.

I told him I had the support of my family. He said I was very lucky for that. (No shit. I still couldn't quite figure out why I had their support.) I explained that I was normally an anxious person, that I had anxiety problems since forever and that I was taking 10 milligrams of Cipralex.

Cipralex is a type of SSRI (selective serotonin reuptake inhibitor) and is commonly prescribed for people with anxiety issues. I got my prescription from my doctor years before. I really couldn't say if it worked all that well but my family and I sure could notice a change in my behaviour if I missed a pill. I turned into a growly, short-tempered bear.

My therapist's advice in the beginning was to slow down. Take things one day at a time. Relax as much as possible and try to stay occupied. To that end, he suggested I participate in relaxation therapy, offered at the same location every Friday afternoon.

Anxiety is fear of the future, my therapist said, and it was important to try to bring my mind from the unknown of the future to the here and now. Relaxation therapy was a six-session course that could be started any time and the instructor taught various ways of relaxing and something called mindfulness, which would help me to stay in the present moment.

I wasn't working. I was feeling rotten about myself and my prospects for a future. I told my therapist I would go.

I ended up going to eight sessions of relaxation therapy at Kelowna Mental Health. Despite my feeling that I had no future and with legal problems hanging over my head, I threw myself into therapy. Every Friday I made the drive into Kelowna to the mental health centre. Every time I put the parking ticket on the dashboard and closed the door, I locked the door of the car. Every time I started to walk away, I would have to stop and relock the door to make sure it was locked. Several times I would do that, walk into the building, then walk back out to press the button on the key fob and hear the reassuring sound of the car's horn announcing that, yes, the car was locked.

There was usually six to eight of us at relaxation therapy, plus the instructor. Each week she taught us a new technique. One week's lesson was on belly breathing, taking in full lungs full of air and slowly breathing out, controlling our breathing in the process. Another week we concentrated on the sounds around us as we let thoughts that popped into our heads float on by, not taking hold.

I enjoyed relaxation therapy a lot. For one hour each week I found myself fully relaxing and, with practice, becoming more focussed on the immediate, less worried about the future.

It was something I started to practice nearly every day, concentrating on my breathing, shutting out extraneous noises and allowing thoughts to drift by without reacting to them. I practiced relaxation even at times when I wasn't necessarily overly stressed, to get in the practice so the technique would be available to me when it was really needed.

Although I started to get good at relaxing, no relaxation therapy in the world would change my predicament. I did something. The police got involved. I could end up getting charged for a crime, which would mean court and possibly jail time. Above all, there was something truly wrong with me. I was a sick, twisted person that hid his thoughts from the rest of the world. At least they were hidden until the Day from Hell when the police showed up at my door.

Chapter 5
Vicious

Starting in junior high school, there was a direct correlation, in my mind, between what I thought and what I was capable of doing. I believed if I thought it, I would do it. I believed thoughts would lead to action.

That's a scary proposition for a teenager who thinks the strangest things. If I thought I might be gay, then I could be gay. If I thought about standing up in the middle of class and screaming my head off, then there was a good likelihood that at some point I would do it. I also believed that other people would, if they knew about my thoughts, draw the same correlation. They would think if I have a bad thought about something, then I was entirely capable of doing that thing. That's the biggest reason why I didn't tell my mom, an older sibling or teacher about my thoughts. I was scared as hell that they'd draw the same conclusion and I'd be sent away to some kind of institution.

Maybe yelling in class wouldn't get me sent to the funny farm, but what about thinking about grabbing a steering wheel and wrenching the car into oncoming traffic? That's pretty serious. Even stealing a chocolate bar was serious when I was a young teenager.

One kind of thought that began in junior high and coalesced into something truly frightening, would have brought me to the attention of the police and those who wear white coats and brandish strait jackets, I was sure. These new thoughts were worse than all of the others that had shown up before. I thought of them as hurt-thoughts and they disgusted me.

I thought about hurting other people and thinking those thoughts hurt me. Every time I hurt people in my mind, it was like stabbing a dagger into me. I would get very anxious. I'd feel sick and scared and, well, hurt.

If my thoughts were candy, these types of thoughts were jellybeans – they came in many different flavours. In addition, they were all violent.

It's lunchtime. In the gym, up above the change rooms and teacher's office are the bleachers. That's where everyone goes to eat lunch or watch intramural sports.

I'm sitting with John. We talk about a girl, who she's going out with this week and the state of our locker-warm sandwiches. Downstairs two teams play volleyball in the gym and we watch the game as we eat and talk.

We wolf down our sandwiches. John says we should go outside before lunch break is over. I agree. We jump up and walk along the aisle toward the stairs. John heads down first and we take the steps at a run, like everyone else in school does. Everything slows down. My vision blurs on the outside until I'm focused on John's back.

My right arm comes into view as it swings toward John. My hand whips forward and slaps John square between the shoulder blades. John's head and torso react swiftly by flying forward faster than his feet. Suddenly John is horizontal, his feet pointed toward me, as his head careens downward toward a step. In slow motion, John's face smashes into the step and several teeth spray from his mouth, along with a good amount of blood in a spurt. His eyes scrunch shut as his head bounces and lands on the next step down. There's blood, dirt, and teeth everywhere.

I stand on a step, frozen. My eyes are wide with fright as I watch John's back receding away from me. He stops, turns and asks, "You coming or what?"

I didn't do it. I thought I hit him and he went forward and smashed into the steps. I really thought it happened this time. Would it? Could it? I might do it next time. What's going to stop me? I've thought it before. Push, fall, smash. Every time on stairs with someone in front of me. I push. They smash. I don't want to hurt someone. I really don't. John was there in front of me, then he was falling toward the stairs and the blood. I keep thinking it and that means I want to do it. Doesn't it? If I keep thinking of doing it then I want to do it. One day I'm going to do it. I pushed him and he fell and he got really, really hurt. I'm so sorry. I don't want this. I don't want any of this. I want it to all go away. It will happen and then John or someone else is going to go face first into the stairs and... Please no. I don't want this! Somebody make it go away! Why do I keep thinking this stuff?

<> <> <>

Hurt-thoughts were a type of thought that first showed up in junior high where someone else got hurt. Strangely, I didn't think about the hurt coming to me; it was always directed toward someone else.

Friends and family members were the two biggest targets of the hurt-thoughts, likely because they were the people I spent the most amount of time with. No one was immune to my thoughts, however. Anyone could be a target. Random people on the street. A kid in a grocery store. A woman standing in line at the bank. Anyone, really.

One thing that hurt-thoughts had in common was I instigated them. Somehow, some way, I ended up being the instigator of the hurt, the beginner of the action that ended up with someone getting hurt.

Another commonality among the different kinds of hurt-thoughts was it didn't feel like just a thought. Many times, it felt like an urge along with the thought. I didn't only think about pushing someone down the stairs. I got an urge to push someone down the stairs. Not only would I often get an urge to do something dangerous or hurtful, but also I could actually see it happening.

That was perhaps the worst part of the hurt-thoughts. Thinking about doing something isn't nearly as scary as actually seeing it unfold before your eyes, even if it's not really happening in the real world. I had a great imagination and I'm sure that contributed to my ability to watch horrible scenes unfold as if they were real.

Countless times, I thought about tripping people. It didn't matter what age they were. I could see maybe an elderly man carrying a bag of groceries out of the store and I'd see myself stick my foot out and trip him up, him flying and his groceries spilling out all over the parking lot. I was responsible for many kids face planting into a sidewalk from a foot stuck in their way. I tripped women, girls, anyone really.

I could be riding my bike down the road and see a young kid walking along the side of the road. I'd get the thought and an urge at the same time to veer my bike over toward the kid and I'd see, actually see, my front tire impale the kid's stomach and watch him fly through the air backward to land on the hard pavement.

As time went on and the thoughts became more frequent and more common, the hurt-thoughts went from the mundane, like tripping someone, to the horrific.

I thought about hitting, pushing, slapping, hammering, stabbing, running over, shooting, maiming, torturing, mutilating and killing people.

My friends died a thousand deaths in my mind before the end of Grade 9. They surely would have died if they met the demise my mind had in store for them. I surely didn't want them hurt. My mind seemed to make up horrible scenarios all on its own and I was a silent witness to the result.

Grade 9s took chemistry in the chemistry lab. It was a cool place of beakers, chemicals stored inside cupboards and a wall-sized periodic table we all had to try to memorize. I loved chemistry and got 100 per cent on the course. The room was both a symbol of achievement and the fountain of many dastardly thoughts.

At times, we had to construct lab experiments at our stations using flasks, tubing and other equipment. Sometimes we had to boil a certain chemical cocktail in a beaker. There were gas jets at each station that could be hooked up by rubber tubing to a burner. When the burners turned on, my mind went into overdrive.

The flame out of the burners could reach eight inches high and I would stop in the middle of an experiment as my mind conjured up body parts of my lab partners being inserted into the flame. I saw myself grab forearms and thrust hands into the flame. More than once, I watched myself, from the inside out, grabbing someone by the head and pushing their face into the flame.

At first when the hurt-thoughts came, I would simply freeze in place, stunned by whatever it was I had just thought. As time went on, I started having conversations in my head about what I had thought and my motives, whether I really wanted that thing to happen or not. It was all hard to process and impossible to put to rest.

Sometimes I would have a fair bit of time to think after a hurt-thought episode to try to figure out why the thought had come and what it meant. It did no good because I could never figure out the answer. Other times one thought would be immediately followed by another and there was no time to think about the first one before I was shocked into thinking about the second.

No matter how hard I tried, I could not figure out where the thoughts came from or what they meant. All I could figure out was that I must be a bad person for having thoughts as terrible as I was having. I concluded early on that no one but a twisted soul could think my thoughts. Normal people didn't think about hurting other people the way I did.

Knives were problematic when I was a teenager. I was fine holding a knife until someone came near me. Then the knife became a big problem. I stabbed my mom hundreds of times when I was a teenager. All in my mind.

If I was in the kitchen and I needed to cut something, I could pull out the biggest knife in our arsenal and use it without a care in the world. If my mom stepped into the kitchen, I'd stab her with it. If my brother or a friend stepped within eyesight, I'd stab them too, but mom was the person around the most so she ended up being punctured more than her fair share.

There was an urge that went along with the thought. It was an urge and a thought, all melded together. I saw myself grasping the knife close fisted and lunging forward with it. I felt the knife hitting, could feel the initial resistance of the skin then feel the skin surrendering as the knife plunged forward.

Sometimes I would manage to continue cutting some cold meat off a roast for a sandwich without flinching. Other times I had to set the knife down on the counter and engage the kitchen intruder in conversation or go get a plate or do anything else, so long as I wasn't holding a big knife while someone else was in the kitchen.

Sometimes I wanted to scream from the insanity of it all.

If you were a cop and you lived in Grand Centre, Alberta in the late 1970s and you were in relatively close proximity to me, you were putting your life in your own hands. At least as far as my mind was concerned. I had this thing about cops when I was a teenager. At least, I had a thing about their guns. The cop had to be close. Real close.

If I was sitting at a restaurant, near the aisle, and a cop walked by, and especially if his gun holster happened to be on the side of him closest to me, I would get the urge to reach out, flip open his holster and grab the gun. The thought would continue with me firing the gun at the cop or at some innocent restaurant patron.

It wasn't only a thought of grabbing an officer's gun. There was an urge too. I felt compelled to do it. It was like a hand inside my body urging me forward toward the deed. It was as if I was drawn to do it. It's difficult to say how mortified that thought made me. There were a hundred different thoughts that would run through my head immediately after.

I would never be able to grab the gun before the cop stopped me. Do I really want to grab his gun? The gun would feel heavy in my hand. It would be light as a feather. Why do I think about this every time a police officer is near? I want to touch the gun. I want to feel the gun. I want to feel how heavy it is. Could I grab the gun? Would he stop me before I did it? I'd get arrested. They would find me and shoot me. They would track me down and throw me in jail. Grab the gun. Grab the gun, touch it, feel it, and fire it. Shoot it. Grab it. No. No!

Like all the other thoughts, I didn't want the hurt-thoughts. I especially didn't want the hurt-thoughts when they involved someone I cared about or loved. It was tough being 13 or 14 and having a close friend and having thoughts about hurting him. It was tough being a young teen and picturing hurting my mom. It was tough period.

Unless the thoughts came one after another, which happened often enough, I would have conversations in my head about the thoughts and why I didn't want to have them. It was like arguing with me inside my head.

On one hand, there was the part of me that thought of the thoughts as horrid, horrible, disgusting and scary. That part wanted nothing to do with the thoughts, wanted them to go away and defended me as not being the type of person who would carry out the thoughts I was having.

On the other hand part of me felt I must be a bad person, even evil, to have the thoughts in the first place. Who but a terrible person has terrible thoughts?

These two parts would argue back and forth. I'd have a thought of kicking a pregnant woman in the stomach and suddenly the two sides of me would be off arguing inside my head. I'd be sweating, my heart would be pounding in my chest, my anxiety level would rise and I'd be scared that someone around me knew something was wrong. I'd want to curl up in a ball and hide.

What I couldn't get through my head was that the thoughts I was having were inside my head. They were from me, involving me. They were therefore part of me. They were me. Weren't they?

Sometimes I felt like I was going crazy by all the self-talk that went on inside my head. In fact, it seemed like sometimes the after-talk that took place when the bad thoughts were finished seemed to take up more time than the bad thoughts themselves.

It never mattered that I never actually carried out any of the hurt-thoughts or any of the other insane thoughts and urges that bombarded me. It didn't matter at all. Logically I could have looked at the situation and realized that, even though I had thought wicked thoughts hundreds or even thousands of times, I never actually carried out the essence of the thoughts. That should have been an indication of what would happen in the future. Having thoughts didn't lead to action.

Nevertheless, each time a thought popped up it was

fresh and new. Each time it was like the first time, full of sorrow, worry, dread and anxiety.

The hurt-thoughts of junior high were the worst kind of thoughts possible. Or so I thought at the time. What my first violent thought was is lost to time but, over time, they got worse. I'm sure at the time I thought striking a friend's hand with a hammer or pushing a stranger's head through a plate glass window was the worst possible thought there could be.

My mind had something else in store for me, a twist on the violence theme that made the thoughts even worse, even more repugnant, even more scary and so, so, devastating.

The sex-thoughts started showing up in junior high but didn't really take off until high school. As the hurt-thoughts were solidifying and becoming a regular occurrence in my head, the sex-thoughts began to intrude their way into my psyche. Like most of the rest of my thoughts, they didn't show up one day in a hail of sorrow. They were insipid, slowly easing into my brain as if to carefully get comfortable before releasing their terror upon me.

Unlike the hurt-thoughts, which were devastating to me right off the bat, the sex-thoughts and their innocuous seething into my consciousness were accepted at first as being the thoughts of a horny teenager. All my friends were teenagers. They were all horny too. I thought it was okay that I was horny, that I thought horny thoughts.

I might be walking down the hallway at school and see a pretty girl in a tight tank top and I would think *I want to take her shirt off and look at her tits.* It was that sort of thing in the beginning and I figured it was very normal for a boy of 14 to think such thoughts, especially about girls of the same age. However, like it was with the rest of my bizarre thoughts, these types of sex-thoughts changed and soon started to show their dark side.

Soon enough girls were not the only target of my sex-thoughts. Boys became the subject of the thoughts too. My friends were often the target of such thoughts but like with the hurt-thoughts, any girl or boy could be the focus of the thoughts.

It made it very difficult that I was having random, firing thoughts about taking boys' clothes off and that I was having thoughts going through my head like, *Am I a faggot?* The complexity of the situation made it extremely difficult at the end of junior high and into high school.

The thoughts changed over time from simply stripping someone to see what their bodies looked like to having sex with them. I did not want these thoughts. I fought the thoughts the best I could, though I didn't have a clue how to go about fighting them properly, since I wasn't about to announce to anyone that I was having the thoughts in the first place.

Then violence and sex intertwined.

The sex-thoughts took on a violent theme and by the time I was in high school I was no longer thinking about just taking a girl's shirt off. I was raping them in my mind.

The thoughts infiltrated themselves into my stream of consciousness and soon enough I'd be thinking about rape, violent rape, or even watching a mind-video where I was actually carrying out the act. Thoughts of a violent, sexual nature weren't limited only to people of my own age. Soon I was having the thoughts about adults too, mostly women and most of them certain teachers I had in high school.

I could be sitting at my desk in class, and a female

teacher would be explaining some concept at the board and, wham, the thought of pushing her down on her desk and forcing sex on her in front of the rest of the class would slam its way into my head.

It didn't help that it seemed like very often when a sexual/violent thought would erupt, I would get a feeling, a sensation, in my crotch. It wasn't as if I'd pop a full boner when a thought came along. Rather it was a feeling like something was happening in my private area. It was proof to me that what I was experiencing, what I was thinking about, was pleasing to me. It was disturbing. My mind always said it didn't like the thought, didn't like what it put me through, but these twinges in my nether regions were like an all too often reminder that I might actually like the thoughts.

Not too far into Grade 10, the sexual thoughts were competing with the violent thoughts for primacy of place. It was like having two unwanted monsters inside by head trying their best to take up most of my attention. I saw myself pushing a male student in front of a moving bus one minute and the next minute saw me raping a female student on the lawn a few yards away.

A teacher I knew from when I went to junior high made the situation so much worse. He wasn't a very good teacher. He spent almost as much time trying to befriend his students as he did teaching.

I was a disc jockey in high school. I played records at school dances, weddings and even bars (I could pass for 18 at 15). One time, for whatever reason, I didn't have wheels to transport my equipment and records to a dance on the weekend. One of my friends suggested I call the teacher from junior high. He had a van. We used the van and the dance went off without a hitch. Borrowing the van led to an invitation to go to a drive-in movie. My friends and I readily agreed. It was cool.

We went to quite a few drive-in shows with the teacher. We even went on Sunday nights, when the porno shows were on. Double feature. One of my friends, who was 18 at the time and allowed into the adult only movie night, would sit in the front of the van with the teacher. My friends and I would hide in the back. We got in every time, free.

It was cool to get into adult only movies but the teacher's behaviour during those nights made me feel creepy and uneasy. He talked almost nonstop about sex. He'd point out a girl walking past the van and say, "Go ask her to come here. Ask if she wants to party. Oh, it looks like she has such nice tits! Go get her. Do any of you know her name? Let's get her in the van and have some fun."

We always laughed at what he said but we never tried to get a girl into the van. It was funny but it was creepy too.

We even partied a few times at the teacher's house. He supplied booze or we brought our own. We'd drink and he'd carry on about girls and sex. It was embarrassing to see this overweight, balding teacher talk about sex in such a disgusting way but I was getting to party and watch porn and it all seemed cool too so I kept going along with it.

I can't remember how long we hung out with that teacher. I don't think it was more than a year. During that year, I slowly had my already skewed sense of sex twisted even more. It was right at the worst time possible, as my mind was coming up with all sorts of disgusting sexual thoughts and images that I couldn't shake.

My grades began to suffer. I was one of the top students

in junior high but by the time Grade 10 rolled around my grades slipped and continued to get worse through high school. It became increasingly difficult to concentrate in class with random thoughts firing off. I started spending more and more time trying to fight the thoughts, trying to rationalize why I was thinking the way I was thinking and trying to convince myself that I wasn't some kind of evil monster who was destined to be locked away somewhere.

I believed I was mentally ill. I didn't think there was any kind of classification for the way I was, but I believed I was evil, wicked, corrupt and ugly. If I was Alice in Wonderland, then the further I went down the rabbit hole of thoughts, the more sure I became that I could never tell anyone about the thoughts. I tried to put on a brave face but inside I was slowly dying.

I never told a soul about the thoughts. I couldn't. I was ashamed of them, embarrassed by them. I truly believed I would be abandoned by friends and family if they knew.

In high school and beyond, I believed the thoughts were a part of me, that the thoughts were me, as much a piece of me as an arm or leg. I was a person who thought horrible, malicious thoughts and that's the way it was. Telling someone about the thoughts would have been to expose the real me to the world. It was something I couldn't bear to contemplate.

As the thoughts became relentless, I took the view that I had to hide them as best I could. I had to go on somehow. I kept going. I did all the usual teenage things. I had friends. I went out and partied. I learned to drive, had my first accident, and bought my first car. I held down a job during high school, which translated into a full-time job after. I suspect on the outside I seemed like a normal young guy.

On the inside, I was being ripped apart.

Then along came the worst kind of thought of all.

It wasn't bad enough that my mind would conjure up pain and suffering for the people around me. It wasn't enough to have thoughts and images in my head about forced, violent sex with people my age and, sometimes, older. No, my mind was able to invoke one more type of thought that beat the others easily in the disgusting department.

Kids began being central players in my thoughts toward the end of high school. They slipped into the same types of thoughts I was already having about teenagers and adults.

I wasn't around kids much when I was in high school or even beyond for that matter. I was the youngest of six kids. I had no younger siblings. Mostly I would see kids like anyone else would see them, at the grocery store, the movie theatre or on the street.

Seeing a kid didn't always bring about a thought that I abhorred. I could never figure out what it was about a certain kid that sparked a bad thought but sometimes seeing a kid would spark one and other times nothing happened.

At first kids were simply another trigger for my thoughts. If I saw a teenage girl and my mind decided it was time for a bad thought then it would happen. The same with children.

I'd walk down the street, a kid would ride his bike toward me and nothing would happen. Then another kid would ride his bike near me and suddenly I had the image in my head of grabbing the kid, throwing her on the ground and taking advantage of her sexually.

As time went on and into my 20s and later, there was a subtle shift in the thought triggers. Adults triggered my violent thoughts less and less. Instead, teenagers and younger kids took over as the primary triggers for the thoughts. As the years went by, teens and younger became the near sole focus of my vicious thoughts.

As with sexual thoughts I had toward classmates in junior high, the thoughts associated with young people also sparked feelings in my groin that were most difficult to ignore. At first the feelings didn't make any sense; they were foreign and bizarre and something to be loathed. Over time, the feelings became more frequent. Very often, I would get a sensation down there. I hated it because it told me that I liked my thoughts. I started to believe what the sensations meant, as I continued to get older, that I was attracted to teenagers and kids. Why else would I get twinges in my groin?

Still I fought the thoughts and I fought the feelings the thoughts brought on. I tried my damndest to shut out the thoughts but they kept coming. Nothing I could do would make them stop. I would sometimes slam the heels of both hands against my forehead, repeatedly, to try to knock the thoughts out of my head. They continued.

There were many times when I would look at a teenager my age or a kid younger than me and I would see them naked in my mind. I knew the teenager or kid in front of me was clothed; I understood that. But in my mind, I could see him or her without any clothes on. I could see their genitals. I could see if they were sexually aroused. It could happen anywhere, any time. I'd be walking down a hallway in my high school and my mind would single out one person and suddenly I'd see that person naked. I could go to the movie theatre and be standing in line for popcorn, glance over at an 11-year-old boy and I'd see what he would look like without clothes.

Other times I would see a naked teen or kid fondling themselves or engaged in sex acts with another person. Sometimes my mind lay out the image or like a mind-video of me performing sex acts with a teen or kid.

One thing I did during those times when nudity and sex overlaid themselves on the image of someone my age or younger (or just younger as I grew older) is I would end up staring at the innocent party. It's as if I would freeze as the images assaulted my mind and my eyes would become totally focussed on the target of the thoughts.

I couldn't react the way I wanted to when the thoughts about kids and teenagers arose. What I really wanted to do was clench my fists and scream at the top of my lungs. I so wanted to do that but I was aware that first, I would attract all sorts of attention I didn't want and second, I might end up having to explain to someone what I was screaming about. That couldn't happen.

There was no way I could sit down with someone and tell about my thoughts, let alone the thoughts about young people. No way. It was a horrifying thought to me that someone would know. So I kept the thoughts buried, locked away inside my head. I continued through life without telling a single person what was happening in my mind. I wouldn't tell. I couldn't tell.

At every stage along the way, as the thoughts progressively got worse and more frequent, I always thought that was as bad as it would get. I couldn't comprehend that the thoughts would become worse or more frequent. They always did. It was like I was on a never-ending rollercoaster going through a horror house in my head, passing more and more disturbing scenes as time progressed.

Chapter 6
Growing Older With Secrets

I grew up and became an adult but the thoughts never left me. Sometimes they would wane briefly but come back with a vengeance to take over my psyche. It was a yin and yang proposition. Sometimes the good outweighed the bad, but then the bad thoughts pushed themselves back to centre stage and I'd have to contend with them.

The thoughts got worse. They were bad in junior high and worse in high school. They were worse in my 20s, worse still in my 30s and even worse in my 40s.

Somewhere along the way, I started to get used to the thoughts. It wasn't that I accepted them as okay or anything. I got used to them because they always seemed to be there. Even in the midst of horror and evil, I sensed some familiarity with the thoughts most of the time. I still got anxious with the thoughts. I still wanted to scream. I just got used to the thought baggage I had to carry around in my head.

When I was in junior high school, my anxiety would skyrocket when a nasty thought appeared and slowly drift back down to a normal level. As I reached adulthood, my background anxiety level stayed high all the time. I was constantly anxious. Nasty thoughts, which were very frequent, didn't spike my anxiety as much because I was always anxious anyway.

As I got older, some of the thoughts and urges I had when I was younger began to wane while others became more pronounced. There seemed to be no rhyme or reason why certain thoughts stuck around and others languished.

All through adulthood, any time I was in a crowd or even a group of people, chances were that I would have the thought and urge to stand up and swear my head off. It could happen in the middle of a boring meeting where the speaker was talking about the latest sales figures or while standing in line at a busy coffee shop. I didn't go to the movie theatre much, but I remember having the urge to stand up and yell every four-letter word there while waiting for a movie to start. There were even times I would get the sensation I was going to do it while standing in line at a busy store with lots of people around me.

The thoughts I had about A having to be done before B happened waned. That particular thought didn't bother me a lot during adulthood.

I continued to have the urge to drive head on into oncoming traffic, especially if what was coming at me was a gravel truck. The only difference between childhood and adulthood with this particular thought was that I was the one doing the driving when I was older. I'd be driving down the highway (it happened more frequently when I was travelling at high speeds), see a gravel truck and suddenly imagine myself twisting the wheel so the front of my car was pointed at the truck. I could actually see the event unfold before my eyes, always ending at the point of impact in my mind.

When I had the visions, the urge, of driving into oncoming traffic, which happened thousands of times, I often wondered if I was suicidal. I wondered if deep down I had a death wish and my preferred method to leave this life was to smash my vehicle head on into a fully loaded gravel truck. The thoughts seemed reckless and suicidal.

Through adulthood, I didn't often get the sensation that I had stolen something but that particular thought came back energetically after the Day from Hell. I'd be standing in line at the grocery store and to my right would be the chocolate bar/gum rack and suddenly I'd get the thought that I had pocketed a chocolate bar. It got so bad that I'd go through my pockets carefully looking for the chocolate bar I stole. I never did steal one apparently, but that didn't make the thought any less disturbing.

I was, several times, in close proximity to a police officer when I was older and, sure as shootin', I'd get the urge to reach out and pull his gun out of his holster. The thought freaked me out as much when I was an adult as it did when I was a teenager.

A new type of thought started up when I was in my 30s. I would be driving a vehicle, hit a bump in the road and suddenly the thought would slam into my head that I had run over someone. My panic level would immediately rise, thinking there was someone hurt and bleeding on the road, or worse entangled with the metal under my car.

Most of the time I was able to forcefully resist the temptation to check and see if I had in fact run over someone. Most of the time. There were a few times when I could not resist. The pull to get out of the car and look was overwhelming. My anxiety level would skyrocket. I hated the thought that I had run over someone with my car. The desire to get out of the car and look around and possibly find out I hadn't run over someone and therefore I would feel better for it, was incredibly strong.

One time it happened on the street behind my house. I backed out of the carport and onto the road. I was careful to turn around in the car to look out the back window. I made sure there were no other cars coming and no one was walking along the side of the road. I backed onto the road, turned around and put the car in gear. I felt a bump through the tires.

Immediately, the thought popped into my mind that I had run over someone. I could see legs sticking out from under the car, a body being dragged down the road. I couldn't stand it. Anxious just short of a total panic attack, I pulled over to the side of the road and stopped. I gripped the steering wheel and tried to breathe.

I got out of the car, fully prepared to find a body behind the car on the road or still entangled under the car. I walked to the back of the car and looked down the road. Nothing. I walked all the way around the car. Nothing. My anxiety level was still very high as I made a second trip around the car. Nothing.

Getting back in the car, I started thinking it had all been fake. I hadn't run over anyone. Then the thought hit me that I didn't check underneath the car. My anxiety rose again.

I got out of the car for the second time. I knew I would look foolish to anyone who happened to drive by, but I couldn't help it. I got down on my hands and knees and looked underneath the car from the driver's side. Nothing. I got up, went to the back of the car and knelt down again. I looked under the car, making sure to peer up at the undercarriage of the car. Nothing. There was no body under the car.

It was as if I couldn't trust my own eyes. I could see there was no body and my mind absorbed that fact but right away there was a part of mind screaming at me, telling me with urgency that there was a body under the car and I had to check again. I had an overwhelming need to be absolutely sure but it's like I couldn't be sure, like my mind wouldn't let me be certain.

I felt sheepish by this point and quickly got back in the car. I put it into drive and started down the road. The thought stayed with me, however. For the remainder of the trip, I could have sworn I had driven over someone on the road behind my house.

Then there were the hurt-thoughts and the thoughts about kids/teenagers. They never left. If anything, they became worse, almost being cemented into my consciousness. I hurt people on a daily basis. The ways I did it varied widely but the thoughts were relentless. They were usually bad but sometimes, like when I was really stressed, they got far, far worse.

So much of my thinking power was taken up by the thoughts that I had a hard time discerning what was real and what was made up by my brain. Although I didn't think I would ever hurt anyone, I couldn't be sure because my brain consistently told me I would by showing me images of what it would be like. Although I didn't do anything with kids, my mind made me believe I was a pedophile through nasty thoughts and images that assaulted me daily.

The hurt-thoughts and the thoughts that made me think I must be a pedophile-in-hiding came in several forms. I would often think a what-if scenario involving another person. Sometimes I would get an image frozen in my head of some awful situation involving someone else. Other times the image would unfreeze and I would see a mind-video of a scene unfold in my mind.

The what-if questions that plagued me came in a wide variety that popped into my head with no notice.

What if I push that person off the curb in front of that bus? What if I stick my foot out and that woman goes flying and her face smashes into the bumper of that car? What if I push that kid's head underwater and hold his head there? What if I grab that young girl and rape her right there by the picnic table. What if I kick that dog so hard his lungs pop out? What if I swing the bat and hit the umpire in the head? What if I plunge this screwdriver into that guy's stomach so hard it comes out his back? What if I turn the wheel and drive right over that woman pushing the baby stroller? What if I turn the wheel and drive right into that crowd on the sidewalk by the bank? What if I try to open the airplane door at 30,000 feet? What if I hold this staple gun up against that woman's forehead and pull the trigger? What if I run over that boy's leg with the lawnmower?

I could get an image of some dastardly deed being perpetrated on other people or an image of some repugnant, vile or horrible situation. I might be in a store and see a boy, 12-years-old and suddenly the image I had isn't that boy wearing jeans and a T-shirt but completely naked, standing in front of me. Instead of wondering what if I tripped someone, I would look at a person and see my foot sticking out and the person suspended in mid-air, just before she crashed to the ground.

The mind-videos were worse. I wouldn't only see an image of something nasty. I watched the scene unfold, like watching a scene from a movie. I saw pain and other emotions on faces, limbs flying around, bones breaking and blood spurting. It was like a horror movie in my head, short-lived, but very intense.

There were times when the what-ifs, the images and the videos would appear for a short time then never again be repeated. Then there were many times when I would be forced to think or watch the same horrid scene repeatedly. Sometimes a situation with a certain person was stuck in my head. I would witness it multiple times a day for weeks. The same image. The same video. The same questions, relentlessly repeating. I thought I would go insane. Some thoughts that I would get repeated hundreds of times. It seemed like they would never stop.

A thought might enter my head once, then come back 10 times over the following day, then not show up for a month, when it slammed its way back in.

I would wonder if I somehow made the thoughts come. Did I consciously think about the thought? Did I somehow trigger the thought to come? I'd question what I had been thinking before the thought appeared and wonder if I had inadvertently made the thought appear.

Most of the thoughts were triggered by seeing other

people or from being in a particular situation. If I saw a kid, I might get the thought of doing something vile with that kid. If I saw an adult, I might think about hurting that person. If I stood in line at a coffee shop, I might get the urge to swear until I was blue in the face.

There were times when I went to bed at night and I would have an evil thought going through my head, then I'd wake up in the morning and the first thought that entered my mind was the exact same evil thought. Did I dream about the thought and end up thinking the same thought for eight or nine hours straight?

Bedtime was a bad time for the thoughts. Though there was no one else around at the time, except for Jackie lying next to me, it was a time when the bad thoughts of the day seemed to replay in my head.

I hated going to bed at night. In later years, I became a night owl, staying up way past any reasonable time for bed. I knew when I went to bed I would end up lying there, assaulted by the thoughts, undisturbed by any distraction like having the TV on. I would be alone, Jackie purring next to me, with thoughts that made me sick and want to scream. I wanted to be good and tired so I would fall asleep quickly and not have to deal with the nightly onslaught.

I thought I was crazy.

Day after day, year after year, the thoughts were a part of everything I did. I would sometimes get a respite from the thoughts, if things were going well in my life. Mostly the thoughts were always there, like an anchor tied to my neck. I dragged the anchor with me everywhere I went.

I thought I was a hideous person. No, I knew I was a hideous person. No one who had these thoughts could possibly be a good person. I tried to be good in my life, be good to my wife, my kids, people I met. I tried to lead a good life, but it never stopped the thoughts. No matter how hard I tried, I couldn't shake the thoughts. Being good was apparently not good enough.

There were times when I would get a single, isolated thought and I would think and think and think.

Why did I think that? Why did that thought go through my head? I don't really want to do that to that boy. No! I don't! But I must because I thought it. I've never done anything like that in real life but I must want to because I thought about it and people don't just think about things like that unless they want to do it. Oh, shit. Why did I think that? Maybe it's a thought like all the other thoughts, it doesn't mean anything, and I'll be fine. I want to do it. I must want to because I thought it. Think it, do it, be it. I don't. I don't want to hurt a kid like that. I can't want to do it because if I wanted to do it I would do it not sit here and think about it all the time because that's all I do is think it. Think it. I think it but I don't do it. I don't want to do it. But this time it felt so real. It felt real. It felt real enough that it felt like I did it. Like I hurt that boy. He doesn't know what I was thinking. He's gone on with his life without knowing what I thought. If they find out, they'll grab me, lock me up and throw away the key. I'll be called crazy and they'll tell me I'm crazy and I'll be locked up with all the other insane people. I wanted to do that to that boy. No I didn't! I didn't want to do it! I don't want to do any of it. I think it. That's all. I think it but I don't do it. I don't. I wouldn't.

I'd have a conversation in my head after every bad thought but only if the thought came in isolation and there was time to have the conversation. There were times when the thoughts showed up rapid fire, like a machine gun, with barely any time in between. I didn't have time to converse with myself. The thoughts would come so fast, so hard, they slammed into my head like having tennis balls tossed at my head by one of those tennis ball-pitching machines. I had no time to react. There was no time to try to work it all out.

The thoughts exhausted me. I often spent days in a zombie state, somewhere half between unconscious and wide-awake. Into adulthood, I was often tired; too tired to play with the kids, too tired to be of much use even around the house.

I would often curl up in a ball on the couch, trying to force the thoughts out of my mind, willing sleep to come. I hated going to sleep but sleep was a respite from the thoughts. I wasn't consciously aware of the thoughts while I slept. Sleeping meant no thoughts, a null place where my mind was at rest.

So frustrated with insufferable thoughts entering my head, I wanted to stand up and scream. Not scream my head off like the thought that made me think about swearing in front of people, but an honest to goodness, I'm really sick and tired of this stuff, kind of scream.

As an adult I kept the secret as well as when I was a teenager. I didn't tell a soul what was going on in my mind, but there were times when I would come close to saying what was on my mind.

"I can't shut my brain off," or "There are too many thoughts in my head," were comments I made. Without further explanation, it was up to Jackie or whomever else I told to fill in the blanks. Likely, they thought I had too much on my mind but surely, they didn't know about horrible, disgusting thoughts running rampant in my brain.

I trusted Jackie implicitly as we grew up together. I met her when I was 21. She was 19. We got married four years later and have been together ever since. There was one thing though that I couldn't bring myself to tell my wife, my best friend. I thought about it. I thought about sitting down with Jackie or my big sister Barb or both and puking out all about my thoughts. I would think about doing it, spewing out all these horrendous thoughts I was having. I also thought about their reactions.

I could not conceive of anyone understanding my thoughts or understanding me. I had it drilled into my brain, from many years of thinking, that not only was I a very bad person for having the thoughts but everyone around me would see me as a bad person. If I told, I would be ridiculed and chastised. People would throw up their hands in disgust. I would be abandoned.

There wasn't a whole lot worthwhile going on in my life except the people in it. They were my jewels, my crowning achievement, being surrounded by people who thought well of me and loved me unconditionally. If I told about my thoughts, all of that would end. My greatest fear was being abandoned by those I loved.

There was also the real possibility that I would run afoul of the police, the courts or the mental health system if I disclosed the thoughts. It was a fear that went back all the way to when I was 11. It was a fear that stuck around, as I got older. The thoughts I was having were crazy, mean, and hurtful. People who have crazy, mean, hurtful thoughts are locked up in institutions for their own good and for the good of the public.

I was friendly with other people but friends were not something I had as an adult. I know part of that was because I didn't want to introduce more people, more triggers, into my life. The other reason was that I always believed that, somehow, some way, my secret thoughts would be exposed and then I would be abandoned by the friends I had. Better not to have any friends in the first place.

My family didn't know what was going on inside my head. I'm sure there were times they figured there was something wrong. I was often moody, withdrawn, acting isolated from other people. I didn't take well to new people, didn't want to go to other people's homes and I usually couldn't wait to get back to the relative security of home if we did go out.

There weren't many times when the thoughts diminished or drifted off. There were times when the thoughts came in terrible waves, like hard surf pounding a shoreline. Those times, the really bad times, showed up when something bad happened in my life. The more stressed I became in the real world, the harder the thoughts worked to make my life miserable.

The first bad thing to happen to me was the loss of my dad when I was 11. It really seemed to start everything off. It was the beginning of a downward spiral that culminated in the Day from Hell.

There was the day I was in the Cold Lake Hospital, preparing for the arrival of my first child. Jackie was having a tough time, had to be induced and, suddenly, the baby was in trouble and she was rushed into an operating room for an emergency c-section. Garrett came into the world fine but it was quite the entrance.

Two and a half years later, Aaron was born and within an hour, a nurse noticed something peculiar with his heartbeat. I left Jackie in her room at one hospital while I took Aaron to the University of Alberta Hospital in Edmonton for an echocardiogram. I walked into Jackie's room several hours later with an empty car seat. Aaron was in the Neonatal Intensive Care Unit being hooked up to all kinds of machines. He had valval pulmonary stenosis, a narrowing of the pulmonary valve in his heart. For six days, Aaron stayed in NICU, among the tiniest of preemies. He had a balloon valvuloplasty done and it did the trick for the time being, opening up his pulmonary valve enough that he could go home.

Eighteen months later Aaron was back at the U of A Hospital for another procedure. This time I carried him into the procedure room and held him down while a nurse tried desperately to poke his arm with a needle to get an IV line set up. He screamed and screamed calling out, "Daddy, daddy," while I had to hold him down. Finally, they gave him some gas and he drifted off into sleep. I set him down on the procedure table and walked out into the hall. I discovered I had a dessert-plate-sized circle of Aaron's blood on my jeans. He bled all over me when they tried to establish an IV. It was such a traumatic time for us all. Thankfully, the procedure worked and Aaron could look forward to a normal life.

At the same time as Aaron was in the U of A Hospital, my mom was in another Edmonton hospital clinging to life. One morning in the spring, she woke up with her legs feeling funny. Three months later, they found a massive, inoperable brain tumour. She died shortly after Aaron's procedure.

My stress level went sky high during these times when the world seemed rotten and poised against me. I was ill-equipped to handle the heightened anxiety. The thoughts took advantage of my lowered resistance by hammering my head constantly.

If I concentrated very hard on a book or a TV show or a movie, I was able to put off the thoughts for a while. It didn't always work. There was one type of thought I had that seemed to put off the bad thoughts better than any other method. I daydreamed and while I was doing so, the bad thoughts often went quiet.

I daydreamed about many things. Sometimes I would pick up a story line from a book, movie or TV show and my mind would take that idea and run with it. Suddenly I'd be thinking about a completely new plot. I'd be in the plot. I'd be almost acting out the script of a story my mind was creating.

I didn't exactly act out the script, but I said the dialogue. If I were in a quiet place by myself, I would really get into the storyline. I would actually say the dialogue aloud, though quietly. The story would unfold in my mind and my lips would move to the dialogue. It was weird and unnerving if someone saw me talking to myself. However, this type of daydreaming did bring some respite from the bad thoughts that constantly assaulted my mind. I welcomed these daydreams.

I never thought sexually about my own kids. For some reason I was spared that particular form of insanity. They were involved, however, in some thoughts of mine as they grew up.

One of the first recollections I have of an unwelcome thought that involved one of my kids was when my oldest was still a baby. He would be lying on the change table, me standing over him ready to change his bum, and I would think, *What if I let go of him with my left hand? Would he roll over and fall off the change table and land with a splat on the floor?* That particular thought ensured I never let go of him for a second when he was on the change table, even when that thought didn't show itself in my mind. Once bitten, twice shy.

Scarier thoughts showed up at bath time. I played second fiddle to taking care of my boys when they were very young. Jackie was much better at it. There were times it would be my turn to bathe one of the boys in the tub.

From very young, back when we put no more than a couple of inches of lukewarm water in the bottom of the tub and the boys were not old enough to sit up, I would get the mind-video/thought of drowning my boys. I could see my hand gently grabbing one of the boys' heads and turning it around until he was face down in the water.

The amount of anxiety that went through my body during those times was incredible. It was like an electric shock from a powerful cattle prod, jolting me into realizing what I had thought.

The other thought I would get at bath time did have sexual connotations but it wasn't a thought of doing something to my boys. Rather it was the thought that I might do something or that I had already done something. It was maddening.

One of my boys would be lying naked in the tub. I'd

have to soap him from head to toe and then, using my hand and some water, rinse the soap off. That meant touching him everywhere. That was a problem for me. Sometimes I was able to wash one of the boys and get it over with without any adverse thought showing up. Other times I'd be washing and one of the thoughts would just show itself.

Did I touch his penis? Yes, I touched him there. Did I like it? Did I do it because he was dirty there or did I do it because I wanted to, like sexually? Did I have to do it? Didn't I already do it? I had a handful of water and I splashed it down on his penis then rubbed. What if I rubbed too long? Was it too long? If it was just for a second then it was to get him clean but what if I did it for too long? Oh shit I don't want to sexually abuse my boy. I don't want to do anything to harm him. Damnit. How long did I touch him there? Was it for a short time or a long time? Was it too long? Did I touch him for too long?

Frankly, there were times when the soap and water didn't exactly come into very good contact with my boys' private parts. Because of the thoughts, I was concerned that something could happen so I'd sort of fake that part of the bathing rather than risk an incident I couldn't handle.

The same sort of thing happened when I encountered my boys at other times. We wrestled a fair bit when they were younger. It was mostly enjoyable but inevitably, a thought would pop into my head that I could do something bad or I had already done something bad.

Same thing if I had one of the boys on my lap. It wrecked many father-son moments when, instead of enjoying the contact with my son, I had thoughts about enjoying the contact for the wrong reason. It would be further exacerbated if I felt a sensation in my groin.

Why did I feel that? Did I feel that? It was a twinge. I'm not supposed to get twinges when my boy is on my lap. That's not right. I must be thinking about doing something to him. I felt a twinge in my crotch, that can only mean one thing, and that thing is evil, demented and twisted. Get him off your lap. Get him off before it's too late.

It's hard to explain how bloody awful I felt having thoughts that involved my kids. They were my kids, little human beings completely dependent on me for their welfare. The last thing I wanted to do was touch inappropriately or hurt my kids. I wouldn't hurt my kids. I couldn't hurt my kids. But my mind kept telling me I did or would or could.

I would also become scared out of my wits when I had a thought that I might have done something inappropriate with my kids. Thoughts of other people finding out and me being shunned, the cops being called or social services being involved mortified me. I didn't do anything wrong. It was that I thought I could have done something wrong that sent shudders through me.

Starting mid-teens, hurt and sexual thoughts were regularly assaulting my brain. My self-esteem suffered. I began to realize that kids around me didn't have the same thoughts I did. They weren't thinking about killing people or raping classmates. They didn't have brains that didn't turn off, that kept running at full speed all day long, involved with wicked thoughts that made them want to cry.

I was alone.

I started to withdraw. I became an introvert, happy to sit off to the side and read a book while my family laughed and joked around in my mom's living room during a holiday. I was actually fairly outgoing in high school, being involved in many school activities, but many times, I just wanted to shrink back and become part of the background rather than steal the limelight.

When I was a teenager, I realized I was different from everyone else. That made me feel bad. That made me feel sad. I thought of myself poorly. I wasn't physically fit enough. I didn't have a girlfriend. I didn't have enough friends. Everyone around me seemed to have a better life than I did.

As I got older, my view of myself continued to slide. I knew other people around me did not have the same, sick thoughts as me and they appeared so much freer to grab hold of life than I did. I was shackled. They were not.

My self-esteem was profoundly affected. Even though I married Jackie in my 20s, I didn't feel I was a good enough husband. We had two kids but I thought my fathering skills were inadequate. Money was always a problem for us. We never had enough. We lived paycheque to paycheque most of the time. We rented and that gnawed at me because if I were any good we would own our own home.

I always felt that I was destined for something big but that I didn't have the balls to get there. I used to daydream about being rich and famous and could even feel how good that would be but the feeling was fleeting.

I was in management since I was 21 but I always felt I should be able to do better. Something held me back from spreading my wings and becoming all I could be. I think it was the thoughts.

Those damn, insufferable thoughts.

Chapter 7
You've Suffered Enough

I was the director of finance for a door-to-door marketing company in 2002. I did not handle the anxiety the job created very well. I found myself in a constantly agitated state. The sheer stress of the job caused my thoughts, the bad thoughts, to go berserk. It got bad enough that in the fall of that year I up and quit. I walked into the boss's office, tossed my keys on his desk and said, "I've had enough."

Around that time, Jackie and I heard that one of my relatives was undergoing treatment for OCD. He was getting disturbing thoughts. Hurtful thoughts. The reaction was swift. He was put on medication and he began therapy.

My knowledge of the disorder at the time was about as poor as the average person's. I thought it had to do with washing your hands a lot, being fastidious and clean.

Still, it made me wonder. If my relative was having disturbing, hurtful thoughts and I was having disturbing thoughts maybe that meant I had OCD as well. Fateful indecision meant I never bothered to talk to him about his thoughts. I should have asked what kind of thoughts he was having, how they manifested and what kind of help he was getting for his condition. I didn't do that.

Part of the reason I remained silent was fear. I was afraid to expose my thoughts to anyone. They were so truly horrible I felt myself a monster and I truly believed I would be abandoned by those I loved if they knew what went on inside my head. My relative may have been having bad thoughts but I really didn't think his thoughts could possibly be as bad as mine could.

Another reason I didn't talk more openly about my thoughts was the thoughts involving children. Surely, they weren't part of some disorder called OCD. I checked out websites about Obsessive Compulsive Disorder. Some of the websites talked about the type of OCD I initially thought about, people washing their hands a lot or having to check a lot.

I found some similarities in stories on the Internet to my own thoughts. Some of my thoughts could be related to OCD. On the other hand, there were so many different kinds that I never found an exact match for my thoughts on any website. I certainly didn't find anyone who had thoughts about children and sex.

Months passed and I found myself thinking about having OCD a lot.

Could I have it? Could I? That site I looked at last month had that post from someone about thinking about pushing people down stairs and I have thoughts like that so maybe I do have it. Then there was that other page I saw that talked about people with OCD having thoughts they don't want, that they just show up. That's what happens. The thoughts pop into my head. That means I have it. I can't have it. I can't. It has to be something else. No page I've been to has been an exact match to me. Or even a close match to me. No, what I think is sick and twisted and it's not OCD. It can't be. What about the thoughts about kids? That can't be it. That has to be something else. Those thoughts are sick, ugly, and hurtful and they can't be Obsessive Compulsive Disorder.

The self-talk inside my head continued unabated. As the years slowly slipped by, there were times when I would suddenly get a jolt and realize that I had been thinking about OCD and whether I had it, for days in a row. It was as if my brain was on autopilot and it thought the thoughts it wanted to without any input from me.

No matter how hard I tried, I could not reconcile my thoughts with what I read on the World Wide Web. Sometimes weeks or months would go by without a Google search, then I'd get an overpowering urge to search OCD again and I'd read page after page on the web and post after post on forums. I never met an exact match to me.

I would often get frustrated and angry at the whole situation. I'd want to scream because I didn't want to think about it anymore. Some days I'd convince myself I did have OCD. Other days I was convinced I didn't have it and I was a hideous person hiding his depravities from the world.

I started working for the local newspaper in the spring of 2003. I'd be working late at night writing stories. I'd be deep in thought about the latest town council decision. Suddenly a thought would appear.

I don't have OCD.

Off I'd go again. I'd be sitting, trying to work and write and organize a story and half my brain was trying to figure out whether I had the disorder or not. It was maddening.

Before I knew it, 11 years had gone by and I realized I had been thinking the exact same thoughts about having OCD for more than a decade. The thoughts were as pervasive, as pernicious, as the harm-thoughts and sex-thoughts.

I was at a turning point. My life had been ripped apart by the arrival of the police at my door, a legal case loomed over my head and there was the unexpected revelation that I had been chatting on the Internet about a most unsavoury subject. I was feeling incredibly low, withdrawn and isolated. There didn't seem to be any reason anymore for hiding secret thoughts and the feelings that went along with them.

Jackie encouraged me to be more open. Above all else, she wanted me to get better. Her encouragement powered me forward to make an admission that ultimately changed my life.

I saw my therapist at Kelowna Mental Health several times before I decided to go for broke. It was the middle of summer in the Okanagan Valley, the sun was shining bright and I found myself in his second floor office.

"I think I might have OCD," I said.

My therapist and I talked about OCD for a time. He admitted he didn't deal with the disorder a lot but he had some experience with it. He rifled through his emails and found one from a co-worker about an upcoming therapy course specific to the disorder. He made a note to try to get me booked in.

The next day I received a call from one of the coordinators of the therapy course. I was booked in for the course, which started in October and ran for two hours, once a week, for nine weeks.

The next week I was back at my therapist's office for another session. "I haven't actually been diagnosed with OCD," I told him. That didn't sit well, since he had me lined up to take the therapy. My therapist excused himself for a few minutes and returned with a note in his hand.

He had walked down the hall and set up an appointment with a psychiatrist working out of the same office. I started getting apprehensive about seeing a psychiatrist.

On one hand, seeing a psychiatrist meant I would finally get a diagnosis and I could end what seemed like an endless torment of thoughts about Obsessive Compulsive Disorder. Finally I could get an answer about at least part of the reason why I had the thoughts I had.

On the other hand, after 10 years of thinking about it, I suspected that although a psychiatrist might tell me I did in fact have the disorder, he might also single out the really, really bad thoughts of mine and point to a different diagnosis. I feared a psychiatrist would tell me I was a pedophile and either a sociopath or a psychopath.

My appointment with the psychiatrist was scheduled for July 29, 32 days since the police showed up at my door with a search warrant.

I was apprehensive but resigned to the fact that he would say whatever he was going to say. I had decided that I would be brutally honest with the psychiatrist. I would answer all of his questions.

I'd never been to a psychiatrist before. Would I get a diagnosis the first appointment? Would there be some kind of formal tests I would have to take? Would there be multiple appointments complete with a couch to lie on and inkblots to look at?

I arrived at Kelowna Mental Health with plenty of time to spare to worry about the appointment. I locked my car, more than once, and went inside. In the waiting room, there was the usual jumble of people waiting for appointments. Some sat still. Others weaved back and forth or had their legs moving up and down like crazed pistons. I began looking at these people differently from the first time.

The people around me were no longer weird, drug crazed people. They were real, ordinary people who needed help. They had addiction problems, sexual abuse problems or disorders I couldn't even begin to understand. They weren't weird at all. They were all there for help. Just like me.

The psychiatrist was not what I expected. My first impression was that he was tall enough to be a basketball player and much too young to be a qualified doctor. He ushered me into his office at the back of the mental health centre. There was no couch for me to lie on in the office, so there went that stereotype out the window. There were two chairs in a cramped office that could have belonged to an accountant.

He was a no-nonsense type of shrink who cut to the chase. There was no talking about my childhood, how long my mother breast-fed me or whether my siblings were overly protective or mean.

The psychiatrist wanted to know what brought me to

see him. I told him I thought I might have OCD. I told him about the various types of thoughts that I had. I told him when I was stressed out, how I would repeat the last syllable of certain words, usually ending in 'ing'. He told me that was called palilalia.

I described when I was younger how I would get the urge to stand up in a classroom and swear my head off. I told him I still occasionally get the urge, but usually in a line-up at a coffee shop or a situation like that. I told him of the thoughts about driving into oncoming traffic, thinking I might be gay and the recently added problem of not believing my car was locked.

I swallowed hard before I told the psychiatrist about the hurt-thoughts I had, like pushing people down stairs, smashing their faces into glass display cases and tripping them. And I told him about the thoughts that made me think I was a pedophile.

The thoughts started sometime after my dad died when I was 11-years-old, I told the doctor. No, I never told anyone about it and never got any kind of counselling or help for it. He shook his head at that.

The psychiatrist wanted to know what my views were about chatting on the Internet in chat rooms that dealt with child sex. I told him part of me was excited by the act but a bigger part was disgusted with the prospect of doing it. I told him that it was more a case of having to do it, not wanting to do it. I was pulled to chat. I had an urge to do it. And after I would chat, I would spend hours and hours chastising myself for doing it, telling myself it was proof I was a bad person.

He asked me if I masturbated while I chatted on the Internet. I told him no, but I had to admit that I sometimes got feelings down there as if I was getting aroused – the same feelings I would sometimes get when I had thoughts about children and sex or adults and sex.

I spent 45 minutes in the psychiatrist's office that day. The time passed in a blink. About 10 minutes before the end of the appointment, he looked at me and said the first of two things that literally changed my life.

"You've suffered enough," he told me. "You have OCD and we're going to do something about it."

I felt lightheaded.

I've suffered enough? That means I've suffered. That means I've suffered up until now. That means there really is something wrong with me. I'm not crazy. I've been suffering.

Then the psychiatrist looked at me again and gave me his second life-changing pronouncement of the day.

"It's all OCD," he said. He explained the thoughts I was having, including about kids, the chatting on the Internet, everything, was a result of the disorder.

I was shocked. I sat there. He might as well have told me I was from Mars for all the sense he was making.

"But how could chatting on the Internet be OCD?" I asked, bewildered.

The psychiatrist explained that sometimes people with the disorder could become fixated on their obsessions. That's what happened to me. Obviously, I needed to stop chatting on the Internet if I hadn't already, according to the doctor, but it was all OCD.

The doctor's words were slow to sink in.

He told me there were several good medications that I could take, all SSRIs, and one that could be taken in combination with an SSRI for better results. I told him I was on 10 milligrams of Cipralex for anxiety. He said that's fine for general anxiety but it needs to be in a higher dose to deal with OCD. He wrote out a prescription to boost my daily intake of Cipralex to first 20 milligrams per day for a few weeks, then 30 milligrams.

The psychiatrist could sense what was going on in my head, because several more times he looked at me and said in a firm voice, "It's all OCD."

With prescription in hand and a dazed feeling in my head, I shook the doctor's hand and started walking out of his office. I turned left and started down the hallway, amazed at what I had been told. "It's all OCD!" the psychiatrist said behind me, loudly. I turned and looked at him, nodded my head, turned around and continued down the hallway.

Robotically, I got to my car in the parking lot and managed to get inside. I was stunned.

It's all OCD. All this time I was suffering. He said I suffered enough. I was suffering. I am suffering. Suffering means there's something wrong with you so there is something wrong with me and it's OCD. Even chatting on the Internet has to do with the disorder. I thought I was a bad person, a sick person, a sicko but my psychiatrist said it's all OCD. What if I'm not a bad person? What if all this time I've been a person suffering but not knowing I've been suffering and instead I've had a mental disorder. Oh my god I have a mental disorder. I am crazy. I'm so crazy my craziness has a name. It's called Obsessive Compulsive Disorder. That's the type of crazy I have. I'm crazy. No, I'm not crazy. I know there is something wrong. I've always known something was wrong except now it has a name and its OCD and I've suffered enough for it, that's what the doctor said. He said you've suffered enough and he ought to know what he's talking about. All this time I've beat myself up, told myself that I'm an evil person, a bad person, a person who has sick thoughts and all this time it's been a mental disorder that's made me think the thoughts I think. Oh my god.

I didn't make it two blocks on the way home before the tears started to come. They were hesitant at first, but once the gate was open, they poured forth, making my vision blurred. I cried only once since the Day from Hell. My emotions stayed buried inside me, but I started to cry like an 11-year-old missing his daddy. I cried big, fat, sticky kid tears. I sobbed as I drove. I should have pulled over but I kept driving. I wanted to get home.

I have OCD. I was diagnosed. All this time I had a mental disorder. I thought that maybe I had OCD but that was for some thoughts, not all the thoughts, because I thought some of the thoughts, the really, really bad thoughts were because I was a really, really bad person. It's all OCD. That's what he said. He said he could help me. There are things that we can do to combat the disorder like taking medications and there's this therapy course coming up. My life could change; my life could be different now that I know I have a mental disorder. What could my life have been like if I had known I was sick and done something about it before? Oh, man I could have had a different life. My life could have been so much better if I had known I had OCD. If I had told someone when I was a kid instead of hiding it. Hiding it because I was afraid and terrified and nauseated by the thoughts. What could I have become if it wasn't for this thing called Obsessive

Compulsive Disorder? Would I have been a better husband and partner? Would I have been a better dad to my two boys? What would it have been like if I had gone through life without the thoughts? Oh man, my past was so screwed up because of this. So much time spent on the thoughts and thinking about the thoughts and thinking about thinking about the thoughts and oh man, I could have had so much better a life if it wasn't for this stupid disorder. It has a name and now I can yell at it. I can scream at it for making my life miserable. My life has been miserable and it's because of fucking OCD.

I was sitting in the Oasis when Jackie came home from work. She walked through the back gate and could tell I had been crying. We sat and talked. I told her everything.

You've suffered enough. It's all OCD. The words of my psychiatrist that caused me to bawl like a baby and the words that would change my life.

Everything changed that day. A small part of me began to realize I was no longer a bad person who was caught. I was a good person with a mental disorder who made a mistake. It was a big distinction in my mind.

Part Two
<> <> <>
Introspection

Chapter 8
The Mental Itch

A little over a month after the police showed up at my house I found myself in mourning.

I mourned the loss of my beloved website, a labour of love I had worked on for several years. It crashed and burned. The police didn't kill a profitable enterprise. The nails were in the coffin long before they showed up. I was distressed that years of my work went down the drain and terrified over what the future held.

For 10 years, I was a reporter in Peachland. I wrote about Peachland for Peachlanders. It started when I wrote several letters to the editor at the end of 2002, to show the owner of the only newspaper in Peachland that I could write. Apparently it worked, because I went to him and asked for work. He agreed. I started slow, picking up some stories here and there. It was a real thrill to see my by-line in the newspaper. Soon I was writing the entire newspaper, covering car accidents, council goings on, community events, everything.

I continued as the only reporter in Peachland for about eight years. At that point, I had enough of the owner of the local newspaper. He apparently had enough of me too because my contract was terminated. I found myself without work but loved being the reporter in town.

The local market had a major regional website that, by all appearances, was wildly successful. Perhaps, I thought, I could step that down a notch and develop a website for Peachland, with all the local news and community events. So, I started up the website, wrote like crazy, learned all about building websites and maintaining them.

The pinnacle of the website came the day in September 2012 when the Trepanier Fire started. Everyone was suddenly on my website, looking for the latest news. My readership shot up and my Facebook page and Twitter feed were abuzz with the news of the fire that threatened little Peachland.

Unfortunately, I wasn't a salesman. Writing good stories and publishing them in a format most people could access wasn't enough. I needed advertising revenue. I couldn't afford to hire a salesperson but a salesperson was what I needed. I concentrated too much on the look of the website, its features and the news and not enough on bringing income in. I kept the website going long after Jackie had enough of my long hours of work and my lack of financial performance.

By the time the Day from Hell came and the police walked into my yard, my news website was on its last legs. I was in turmoil.

It was my baby. I gave birth to it. I made the website look the way it did. I tweaked it constantly. I kept adding fancy features to the website. I reported like crazy. I outperformed all competitors for the Peachland market. It didn't matter. From the get go the enterprise was almost doomed. No matter how I tried, I could not make money. I was under tremendous pressure to not only make the website succeed, but to also bring home a decent paycheque that would show all the incredible number of hours I put into the website were worth it. Every month that went by with little or no pay stressed me out further.

I always seemed to be under pressure, often self-induced. The two years or so that I ran the website were both exciting and miserable. It was exciting to be in a new business venture but miserable to eke out an untenable existence off my labours. The stress of working long hours on the website with little financial reward took its toll. I put on a brave face but I was under a lot of pressure and that stress made my OCD worse.

I would go to a community event to gather information and photos for a story and find myself in the midst of a storm of violent and sexually based images and thoughts. I'd go over the thoughts in my head repeatedly, trying to figure out what they meant and what they said about me as a person. I'd fight through it as best I could, write the story and publish it. I'd work and not get a paycheque. I was stressed every day. My OCD got worse.

It was during that time, while I wallowed in a pit of mental disorder despair, that I started chatting on the Internet about some of my sexual thoughts. I found other people who thought the way I did. I thought this was who I was.

I had no concept of right or wrong. I had spent nearly 40 years keeping my thoughts a secret from those I loved. I truly believed I would be abandoned and perhaps committed, if I told anyone about my thoughts. The only outlet for the nasty, disgusting thoughts was a place on the Internet I found where disgusting was the norm and all manner of depravities are openly expressed.

My website failed. I mourned.

I also mourned my childhood and even my adulthood. I felt robbed by a disorder I didn't really yet understand. I spent many hours in the Oasis, away from the public and the people who were used to seeing me all over town, thinking about how my life could have been vastly different if not for the disorder.

What kind of life could I have had if it wasn't for OCD? What would my childhood, in junior high and high school, have been like if I didn't have those horrid thoughts running around inside my brain? What kind of jobs would I have had if not for the thoughts? How relaxed would I have been after a day's work if I hadn't spent half the day or more thinking about the dreaded thoughts? How much better of a husband and a father would I have been if not for Obsessive Compulsive Disorder? Would I be rich by now? Would I be famous? Would I have a comfortable job, a nice house, toys like everyone else, and many friends?

In the summer of 2013, I wasn't convinced that OCD was at the heart of all my problems. I had doubts.

Part of me wanted to believe my psychiatrist wholeheartedly. I desperately clung to the belief that my abhorrent thoughts were caused by a mental disorder. It would explain a lot. He was, after all, a real psychiatrist and he had diagnosed me with having OCD. When he said, "It's all OCD," that had to count for something.

Another part of me was wary and doubtful about my psychiatrist's diagnosis. I could almost buy the explanation for most of my bad thoughts, especially those that, over the 11 years I looked into the disorder, matched up with types of the disorder I knew. I had seen people talk about thinking they had run over someone in their car and that was a type of thought I had so it seemed reasonable to think it was caused by OCD. There were other thoughts where I relatively easily bought into the OCD explanation, like thinking about driving into oncoming traffic and even some of the hurt-thoughts I had. I had seen mention of those types of thoughts before and I had no problem believing they were caused by OCD with me.

The one type of thought I had trouble believing was caused by the disorder was the hurt and sexual thoughts involving children. I couldn't wrap my head around the idea that I had chatted on the Internet about a despicable subject and that it had its roots in the disorder. The hurt and sexual thoughts involving children had been a big part of me since I was about 15 and I had spent a lifetime convincing myself I was an evil pedophile because of them.

To compound the problem, in the months immediately following the arrival of the police at my door, I had an urge, an overwhelming urge, to go back on the Internet and continue chatting in that dark place.

Having that urge reconfirmed I must be a bad person because who but a pervert would think about doing what had already gotten him into trouble? Then again, the urge to chat more was very much like the urge I had to get down on my hands and knees and check underneath my car because I was sure I had run over someone. It was exactly the same feeling.

I steadfastly refused to go back to chatting, though the urge to do so was powerful.

Even though I had been offered not only a diagnosis but also a reason for being the way I was, I couldn't easily come to terms with the belief that it was all OCD. I was diagnosed by a professional. He told me that I had this particular disorder and my problems were because of it. But I didn't just have the disorder. My thoughts were from the dark side of OCD. I didn't just have unwanted thoughts. I had vicious thoughts, wicked thoughts.

I may have been without a job, without a source of income, without a life as far as I was concerned, but for Jackie life had to go on.

The day the cops came was Jackie's day off. The next day, the day I came home like a stray cat, Jackie took off from work. After that, she had no choice. She had to go to work. My website wasn't bringing in a sustainable income and I couldn't put any more effort into it. I had to deal with pending legal problems and a mental disorder I only recently discovered I had.

Jackie had to go to work, no matter if she would have preferred to crawl under a rock. Somehow, Jackie put on a brave face and continued on. While I spent time in the Oasis in mourning, thinking and trying to sort things out, Jackie had to go out and be part of the big, wide world. I don't know how she did it.

She met up with people we knew and had to answer the inevitable question, "How are things going?" Jackie had to go into stores; some of the same stores that were visited by the police when they were out searching for me the day I disappeared. She had to talk to cashiers and store owners. Who knew whom she would bump into at a store or on the street? Peachland was a small town and like most small towns, everyone at some level knows everyone else. Many people knew me because of my reporting. Quite a few of them knew Jackie was my wife and that could lead to questions from people about how I was doing.

Jackie was the personal assistant to a family in Peachland, a job that includes cleaning their house and a myriad of other responsibilities. She also cleans five office buildings.

Family friends kept coming to our house. It wouldn't have sat well with Jackie to cut off contact with the outside world. People showed up and there would be jokes and loud voices and laughing. I would say hi and either sit in the living room and watch TV or slip out to the Oasis and sit and think.

Jackie is my soul mate. She was very strong after the police left. I'm sure she nearly fell apart at some points but somehow she found the inner strength to keep moving, putting one foot in front of the other. She found the energy to go to work every day. She found the fortitude to meet people on the street. And she always had love for me.

Jackie saved me by leaving the porch lights on and she was, bit by bit, saving me as I faced my greatest challenge, coming to terms with a mental disorder. I didn't think I could go on without Jackie. I leaned on her a lot and looked to her for encouragement and a shoulder to lean on. Part of me couldn't understand how she remained by my side given what I had done but another part realized it was simply because she loved me and valued our relationship above all else. I loved her back. I loved Jackie and my boys and my two big sisters who stood by my side. It felt like that was all I had but it was enough to keep going.

We had no idea what was to happen after the police came to our house. We heard nothing from anyone and the waiting nearly killed us. Every night we would sit in the Oasis and talk about what wasn't happening, what we thought it meant and what might happen in the future. We waited and waited.

Immediately after my first appointment with my psychiatrist, I took the prescription change to the pharmacy and began taking the higher dose of 20 milligrams of Cipralex. I was on that dosage for two weeks and then it was raised to 30 milligrams daily.

I saw my psychiatrist every couple of weeks in the beginning. It was less a time to talk about OCD and more a time to monitor my reaction to the medication changes.

At first, nothing happened. SSRIs take a while to build up in a person's system. I was already taking 10 milligrams of Cipralex before so I already had it in my system. I wasn't sure what the change to 20 milligrams then 30 milligrams would exactly do.

My psychiatrist seemed confident in his choice of medications. He said I should notice a difference in a few weeks but he didn't really go into what kind of change I would experience. By the end of August, I noticed I was feeling different.

The change came on very slowly.

The police had shown up at my house on June 27. The month of July, I was a basket case. I was barely hanging on by my nails. All I could think of at the time was that my life was over and that I had no future. I was depressed. I was lower than low. I felt guilty, ashamed, embarrassed and lost.

Sometime toward the end of August, I noticed my mood starting to change. It was as if I was previously covered in a deep, thick, dark blanket and it was very slowly being lifted so I could see the light from outside. It was very tentative and slow going.

I began holding my head a little higher. The world didn't seem to be the dark, cold place it was a little while ago. The world actually started looking pretty good. Soon I was going to stores again and talking to people. At least I was saying, "Hi," to people.

I remember driving down Beach Avenue, the main drag of Peachland that hugs the shoreline of Okanagan Lake. The hanging baskets of flowers the town puts out every year were more brilliant, fuller of life than before. Along the lakeshore runs a waterfront walkway and between it and the road are various shrubs and flowers. They were more alive than they were a few weeks before. The colours were more vivid.

In fact, our back yard, as cute as it was as our little Oasis, was more radiant and dazzling than ever. I'd wake up in the morning and I couldn't wait to get outside. I'd sit in my chair and look at the yard – the hanging baskets full of petunias, the snapdragons painted bright yellow, pink and red in the back garden.

I found myself doing something I had not done for as long as I can remember… sitting there, staring at the flowers or perhaps a butterfly lazily fluttering in the back yard, without a thought in my head.

I never could concentrate very well on a TV show or

movie unless the thoughts decided to be quiet that night and I was intent on watching the show. By the end of August, I'd finish a show on TV and suddenly realize that I had actually focussed on and watched an entire hour of TV without one errant thought popping into my head. It actually shocked me when it happened.

Jackie noticed a change too. Our nightly routine, after she returned home from work, was to sit in the Oasis and talk about the day, what happened, who we met, how we felt. She started to notice that when she talked my eyes were on her. They were totally on her.

For the nearly 30 years she had known me, I often seemed preoccupied when she talked to me. It was as if I had something else going on in my mind and I wasn't all there when I was listening to her talk.

That changed dramatically near the end of August. I was focusing on her, on what she was saying, on her words, on the meaning behind the words. My eyes would go to her when she started to speak. They would stay on her as long as she talked. It was a marked difference in my behaviour.

At the beginning of September, two months since the Day from Hell, I saw my psychiatrist. I was on 30 milligrams of Cipralex. He asked me for an honest assessment of my OCD thoughts. I felt like a kid about to show his parent a good report card. I was excited. I was giddy.

"Sixty per cent reduced," I told him.

It sounded like such a big number and it was. In a little over a month, my bad thoughts had shrunk by about 60 per cent. It was incredible. I could barely believe it.

I explained to my psychiatrist that I had many moments during a day when I didn't have the thoughts running through my head. I had long stretches with no thoughts. What was even more incredible is that the thoughts getting through seemed weaker. They still hit but they didn't hit with as much force.

My psychiatrist was pleased. Then he suggested we change my medication and try to get the 60 per cent number higher. He wanted to put me on Rispiradone, a different kind of drug that is sometimes taken in combination with an SSRI for the treatment of OCD.

Rispiradone, as it turns out, was originally prescribed as an anti-psychotic and he was quick to point out that that didn't mean because I was going to take it that I was psychotic. While SSRIs affect levels of serotonin in the brain, Rispiradone affects the levels of dopamine and other neurotransmitters. It works as good for my disorder, my psychiatrist told me.

I had to go in for an electrocardiogram at the hospital before I could start taking Rispiradone. One of the side effects of the drug can be an irregular heart rhythm. My psychiatrist wanted a baseline of my heart before beginning the new drug. It would be best to take the drug at night, since it had a tendency to make people drowsy at higher doses.

I started taking one milligram of Rispiradone daily. Unlike an SSRI, which can take weeks to build up in the system, this new drug began working very quickly. Within a week, I started to notice a big difference in my mood. In some ways, the change was bigger than when I started taking the higher dose of Cipralex. If I was relaxed on the higher dose of Cipralex, I was downright serene on Rispiradone. My spirits lifted higher than I could ever remember them being. I felt at peace, something I had long sought but never found.

I couldn't believe I was feeling that good. Less than two months before I felt my life was over. I had little to live for. Now I was running around the house, cooking meals and cleaning like it was nobody's business. In fact, my energy level shot up shortly after starting to take Rispiradone. One night in the fall of 2013, it hit me like a ton of bricks.

I spent the day cleaning the house but it felt like I could do more. And more. I was sitting in the Oasis with Jackie. It was starting to get dark outside and I told her I thought something was wrong. I couldn't sit still. I wanted to jump up and do something. We talked and talked. It got to be late and I told her I could, right then, go in the house and reorganize all the cupboards. Better yet, I could take a pair of scissors and cut every blade of grass on the lawn, one at a time. I wouldn't have minded a bit.

Where the energy was coming from, I didn't know but that night concerned me. I had never been like that. Usually, I was a couch potato at night, barely moving except to go outside for a cigarette or to get another cup of coffee. Suddenly I had all this energy, like it was all pent up and I needed to release it right away.

It was such a strange feeling to have so much energy. Was it some kind of side effect of the Rispiradone? I had already experienced one side effect of the drug. Soon after taking it, I started moving my legs all the time. I'd be sitting watching TV or be in my chair in the Oasis, and I had this incredible urge to move my legs. It was as if the muscles wouldn't sit still. I had to move them and stretch out to give them some relief.

My psychiatrist told me the restless leg thing would probably go away and it did. However, I was concerned about all the pent up energy I was suddenly experiencing.

I visited my psychiatrist in the fall of 2013 and told him about the energy thing. I told him I thought I was turning manic. He chuckled. He asked me how long these manic episodes lasted. I told him hours. He chuckled again.

Real manic episodes, it turns out, last for five days or more, according to him. Oh.

My psychiatrist suggested the real reason I suddenly had a whole lot of energy is that my mind was free. It was no longer working hard on OCD thoughts. That translated into energy unlike anything I had ever felt.

He then asked me how I was doing on one milligram of Rispiradone in addition to the Cipralex. I had to admit the thoughts had subsided again. My head was quiet. Much more quiet than it had ever been, certainly, since I was young teenager.

"Down by 70 to 75 per cent," I said. That pleased my psychiatrist but it pleased me more.

My psychiatrist had one more trick up his medication-prescribing sleeve. He upped my Rispiradone to one and a half milligrams daily, one milligram at night and a half a milligram in the morning. The result, as I had come to expect, was great. The extra half milligram ended up increasing the rate of decrease of my bad thoughts to about 80 per cent.

My psychiatrist pronounced that I was a textbook case. My reaction to the SSRI and anti-psychotic I was prescribed exactly matched what the literature said should be expected, according to the doctor.

The remainder of the thoughts that were still getting through – and there were still quite a few, would be dealt with when I took the therapy course held in October. I was looking forward to taking that course and learning how to deal with the rest of the awful thoughts that had kept me a prisoner of my mind for so long.

I began to research Obsessive Compulsive Disorder again. I spent more than 10 years bouncing back and forth between thinking I had the disorder and believing I didn't. During that time, I researched the hell out of OCD but little sunk in. This time was different.

Researching didn't come with an urge to prove or disprove anymore. In the fall of 2013 I was more relaxed than I thought possible and inquisitive. I wanted to know about the mental disorder I had. I was still not convinced that the pedophilia thoughts I was having were caused by OCD. My internal jury was still out on that one but I was on board with the rest of my thoughts being caused by the disorder.

Obsessive Compulsive Disorder is a disorder that includes obsessions and compulsions.

Obsessions are intrusive, persistent and uncontrollable thoughts, images, impulses, urges, worries, doubts or fears, or a combination of them. These are the unwanted thoughts I had, the ones I wished I could get rid of. The thoughts are disturbing and significantly interfere with life. They are incredibly difficult to ignore and they cause distress. And they are repetitive.

Compulsions are behaviours, actions, rituals or mental thought rituals performed by the sufferer to try to alleviate the distress caused by obsessions. They are performed repeatedly but each time they only reduce the distress temporarily and, it has been found, they actually serve to reinforce the original obsession, turning a bad situation into an endless, worsening cycle.

In all my research of Obsessive Compulsive Disorder, I have never found a more profound explanation of the disorder than one given by my psychiatrist to me during one session when I invited Jackie along to observe.

"OCD is like a mental itch that has to be scratched," he said.

I found that explanation truthful and insightful. That's exactly what it felt like for me. Every time an obsession struck, it felt like it had to be dealt with, like an irritating itch somewhere on my body. I just had to scratch it.

It explained why, after having the thought and image of pushing a kid down the stairs that I would spend minutes or hours thinking about the situation and whether I really would do it or not. The thought/image was the itch and going over it in my head was the scratch. Itch and scratch. Obsession and compulsion.

During that same session, my psychiatrist explained to Jackie that people with OCD do not choose the obsessions they have. For whatever reason, and the jury is definitely out on this one, sufferers are stricken with different obsessions or combinations of obsessions.

I was pleased to discover that obsessive thoughts are not brought on voluntarily. I often wondered if I was somehow responsible for thinking up my obsessions but it turns out they were completely beyond my control.

I did however realize the thoughts were mine. I didn't blame them on some outside force or person. That gets into the realm of psychotic or schizophrenic. At the same time, I saw why I would get so frustrated over my own thoughts, since they did indeed come from my own mind. Before I realized that I had a mental disorder, I was convinced it was me that was generating the bad thoughts, that I was actually capable of carrying them out.

My obsessions became clear to me, at least for most of them. Thinking of driving into an oncoming gravel truck was an obsession. Imagining standing up and swearing in class or in a coffee shop line-up was an obsession. Thinking I had stolen a chocolate bar at the grocery store checkout was an obsession. So was imagining pulling a cops gun out of his holster. They were all obsessions.

Compulsions weren't so easy to figure out. I didn't have outward compulsions like many people. Take the stereotypical sufferer who has obsessions about cleanliness and contamination. The compulsion might be to wash his hands. The obsession comes back and the compulsion (washing hands) happens again. And again and again and again. That's easy to understand. I didn't wash my hands more than the average person did. I didn't tap walls or turn around three times every time an obsession struck. What were my compulsions?

I figured out most of that question after some more research. I learned by scouring the World Wide Web that one of the biggest compulsions is not a physical, out in the open kind, but a hidden, in the mind one. It's called ruminating.

To ruminate means to think deeply about something without coming up with a satisfactory result. To go over something repeatedly in your mind.

When I saw ruminating raised as a compulsion it clicked in my head. That's what I did, whether I thought about driving my car into oncoming traffic or thought about smashing a kid's face into a plate glass window. I'd ruminate. I'd go over the obsession, as it turns out, in my mind, repeatedly. I'd question why I would think that, what it meant and whether I was a bad person. I'd do it constantly.

With the understanding of what obsessions and compulsions were, I started looking at my past through a different, more knowledgeable lens. I realized that there were many days in the past nearly 40 years when I had spent hours and hours and hours on compulsions, ruminating endlessly in my mind. In addition, I had to admit that there were many days when I faced dozens of obsessions and, on the worst days, I was assaulted by hundreds of them.

Throw in the daydreaming sessions I had frequently and my mind was literally occupied some days every minute of every hour. It's no wonder I had trouble concentrating. No wonder I couldn't focus.

It's a wonder I didn't go insane.

Chapter 9
Taking Stock

I continued to see my therapist at Kelowna Mental Health throughout the fall of 2013. In October, it was time to start going to therapy. The OCD Treatment Group is held once a year in Kelowna. Up to 10 people can attend the group but when I arrived on my first day, only four of us were there. There were two instructors, one of which was a psychologist.

One instructor said it was to be expected that not everyone who signed up for the treatment group would attend. Some people simply aren't ready to take the next step, she explained.

I never attended any kind of group therapy before. After the success I achieved with medications, I was determined to learn all I could about the disorder and how to treat it. I wanted to know how to deal with the disorder that held me in a stranglehold for nearly 40 years.

At the same time, the idea of sitting in a group of strangers and actually talking about my thoughts was unsettling. I kept my thoughts a secret for four decades and only recently shared them with my psychiatrist and my family. I was uneasy thinking I'd have to open up to people I didn't know.

The people running the treatment group obviously knew opening up to strangers could be a problem. The first two sessions, instead of being about describing our most private thoughts, were all about learning about OCD.

Somewhere between one and three per cent of the population will get Obsessive Compulsive Disorder. That was a shockingly high number.

If the average of two per cent is used, that's 700,000 people in Canada, more than six million in the United States and 140 million worldwide. In my little town of Peachland, population 5,300, there would be more than 100 people who either have or will have OCD. The disorder affects people from all walks of life. On average, it begins in the late teen years, although it can develop in people much younger.

Some people with OCD experience mild symptoms, while others have such severe cases that they spend nearly every waking moment working on obsessions and compulsions. Without treatment, the disorder tends to get worse as time goes on.

It turns out that everyone has intrusive thoughts at some point. Whether an impulse to jump off a tall building or train platform or thoughts of an accident or harm coming to a friend or family member, nearly everyone has thoughts they wish they didn't have. The majority of the population simply disregards such intrusive thoughts, attaching little meaning to their occurrence. People with OCD attach meaning to the thoughts, are disturbed by them and cannot get rid of them easily.

The exact cause of the disorder is not known. There is growing evidence that points to abnormal metabolism in certain areas of the brain. There is some evidence that sufferers have an abnormality in the neurotransmitter serotonin. The jury is still out on whether genetics is mainly responsible or if environment is an influence.

The instructors also introduced us to the wide variety of OCD types. There are aggressive obsessions, contamination obsessions and obsessions related to sex, hoarding and saving, religion, symmetry and exactness and a whole raft of miscellaneous obsessions that don't fit into any of the main categories. In addition, compulsions can relate to cleaning, washing, checking, repeating, counting, ordering, arranging, hoarding, collecting, confessing, mental rituals, touching, tapping, rubbing, superstitions, ruminating, reassurance seeking and others.

One of the first things I did as a result of group therapy was to complete the Yale-Brown Obsessive Compulsive Scale (Y-BOCS), which is probably the most recognized format for figuring out the severity of OCD in an individual. By the time I sat down at the table in treatment group, I suspected the severity of my disorder (pre-medications) had been quite high.

The Y-BOCS asks the sufferer to rate, on a scale from zero to four, attributes of obsessions and compulsions experienced. There are five questions for both obsessions and compulsions: time spent, interference from, distress of, ability to resist and control over (obsessions and compulsions).

I carefully answered the questions on the Y-BOCS, which was included in a package of forms and handouts received on day one. When I filled out the form, I specifically filled it out as if I was answering the questions four months previously – before I started on medications for OCD.

Totalling up the answers on the Y-BOCS I rated myself as 34 out of 40, 40 being the most extreme type of OCD. I had a severe to extreme case of the disorder. Had I filled out the Y-BOCS based on the way I was handling my situation in October 2013, I would have rated far lower because of my excellent response to medications.

We learned on the first day of the OCD Treatment Group that we would be learning Cognitive Behavioural Therapy (CBT) with an emphasis on Exposure and Response Prevention (ERP).

CBT is a whole group of specific techniques that can be employed to change the way people think and behave and, for the OCD sufferer, lessen anxiety. ERP is a type of CBT that focuses on exposing a sufferer to an obsession and then practicing not responding to the obsession. In other words, ERP is all about not performing compulsions.

My instructors talked a lot about compulsions. In the short term, performing compulsions can relieve the distress caused by obsessions. But compulsions only temporarily reduce the distress caused by obsessions. The relief doesn't last. Then the obsession comes back again, requiring more compulsions to be performed. In fact, the compulsions actually reinforce the obsessions, making them stronger in the future.

It took me a bit to figure it out but in my case I could see that all the compulsions I had performed over nearly 40 years did nothing to eliminate the thoughts I wanted to be rid of. My compulsions were mental. Ruminating was the big one. It might have reduced my anxiety level for a short time but another obsession would hit and the whole thing would start again.

ERP is all about not performing compulsions. At first, not performing compulsions results in a sharp spike of anxiety that takes a lot of time to return to normal levels. Over time, as research shows, repeated exposures with no compulsions performed causes anxiety to reach lower and lower levels. The time it takes to return to normal shortens. With enough ERP practice, the sufferer should expect nothing but a hiccup after an obsession.

Over the course of nine weeks, the four of us in treatment group would put into practice Exposure and Response Prevention.

Before we could get into ERP, we had to make a list of our obsessions and compulsions. This was my homework early on in therapy. I thought it would be relatively easy to make a list of the thoughts that had bothered me for so long. It ended up being like having a tooth pulled without freezing.

There were so many thoughts in my head over so many years it was difficult to list them. I still hadn't reached the state where I was fully convinced all of the bad thoughts were OCD, so I was hesitant to put down all of the thoughts.

Making the list was especially anxiety provoking because it made me sit down and think, really think, about what had been going on in my mind since I was a boy. I forced myself to think about the thoughts I had tried to bury and push away. It took me several distressed filled nights to complete the list. Eventually I ended up with a list of 17 obsessions and their corresponding compulsions. I was exhausted and overwhelmed by the time I completed the list.

Most overwhelming was not the sheer number of obsessions I had dealt with for nearly 40 years. It was the realization how much of my time and brain power those obsessions, and their corresponding compulsions, took up.

There were days when I would have hundreds of obsessions. I could have dozens of obsessions about hurting people and dozens more about violent sexual themes, all mixed with dozens more from the wide variety of obsessions. I had to admit there were many days when my mind was nearly fully involved in obsessions, thinking about obsessions and performing compulsions. On those days, I lost myself. I didn't know which way was up, what was right, what was wrong, what was true and what was false.

My disorder got worse over time. It was awful when I was a teenager but it got worse as I got older. Toward the end, I was numb to it all. I dragged myself through days of mostly violent, sexual intrusive thoughts that wouldn't let up.

I came to the realization that the fruitless exercise I went through for more than 10 years, trying to figure out if I had OCD or not, was in fact OCD at work. I would spend hours and hours over days and days, thinking about the disorder and trying to figure it out, trying to come up with a definitive answer. I never could. That was a compulsion.

Jackie was upstairs in our bedroom, watching TV. I went up to her.

"I need a hug," I said.

We embraced. I told her what I had done was one of the hardest things I had done in my life. In order to make a list of my obsessions and compulsions I had to relive the thoughts. It was terrible.

I told Jackie about the list. "I don't know how you lived like this," Jackie said. She was shocked to find out how many unwanted thoughts I had and how intrusive they were.

For the most part the compulsions I performed were mental and involved ruminating. The obsessions ranged from having to do A before B happened to thinking I stole something in a store to thoughts of children and abuse.

I had to order the obsessions on the list according to how much anxiety each obsession caused. To do ERP we wouldn't want to start with something too low on the list (too easy to deal with) or something too high on the list (too challenging at first).

The lowest obsession on my list was ordering or arranging things in a particular way until they felt right, which barely gave a rise to my anxiety level. The highest obsession was children and abuse, which rated nine out of 10 on the anxiety scale.

One of the problems I had with the whole listing and rating exercise was that, by the time I began treatment group, most of the obsessions that used to cause me such grief were shadows of their former selves due to the medications. My obsessions were in fact 80 per cent better than they had been. I didn't see how I was supposed to attack a particular obsession if it didn't bother me very much anymore.

One obsession that gave me a headache was the persistent thought that I hadn't locked the car when I went out somewhere. It was the latest obsession to strike me, having only shown up a few months before. For some reason it wasn't responding to the medications like my long held obsessions. It became the obsession I would practice ERP on first.

Actually practicing ERP was straightforward. To do it properly, I exposed myself to the obsession and then resisted or simply did not perform the compulsion.

For months, every time I parked the car I had to lock the car multiple times. Once was never enough. I pressed the button on the key fob and heard the horn confirm the car was locked. I started walking away and suddenly I would get the thought in my head that I hadn't locked the car. I'd have to lock it again. Sometimes this would go on for three or four times or more before I walked in a building.

My new task was to lock the car once. It sounded easy. On the first day of my attempting ERP, I drove to a grocery store. I parked the car, got out, and got my shopping bins out of the trunk. I had the keys in my hand. I purposefully pressed the lock button on the key fob twice. The car horn beeped to let me know the car was locked. I pocketed the key fob, turned and started walking toward the store.

I didn't get 10 feet before the thought popped in my head.

I didn't lock the car.

I stood, frozen, in the grocery store parking lot.

I did lock the car. I for certain pressed the button twice and heard the horn beep. I did lock the car. Am I sure? Am

I sure I locked the car? I need to lock the car again.

It was crazy how anxious I got. The urge to grab the key fob from my pocket was overwhelming. There was nothing valuable in the car, nothing worth stealing. It didn't matter. This big, fat thought was front and centre in my mind and it wanted me to lock the car again.

I let out a sigh and started walking toward the store. The whole way to the store and for quite some time inside the store, the thought was screaming inside my head, demanding I go back and lock the car. It took about 30 minutes, but my anxiety level eventually came down.

Over the next week I practiced not locking my car more than once every chance I got. Every time I parked in a parking lot, I made sure to only lock the car once, regardless the screaming thought in my head. Sure enough, over time, my anxiety level went down a bit each time and the length of time it took for it to recover to a reasonable level shortened. Within a week, I could lock the car, pocket the key fob and carry on with my day with barely a blip registering in my anxiety level.

When I worked on the list of obsessions and compulsions, I was thinking about all of the bad and weird thoughts I had since I was 11. I wrote down as many as I could think of but frankly one of the obsession/compulsion combinations didn't really fit. I was thinking that daydreaming was an obsession/compulsion combination because I would get a thought and then I would play out some kind of fictional scene to go along with it. I thought the playing out sounded like a compulsion. Once I wrote it down along with the other thoughts I had I wasn't so sure.

For one thing, there was no anxiety associated with the

situation when I daydreamed. Unlike the thought of stealing a chocolate bar, which caused a big spike in my anxiety, there was no anxiety spike before or after daydreaming. There could be anxiety associated with daydreaming, but only if I was caught talking to myself. It happened on occasion when I whispered the dialogue and someone would see me. Then there was anxiety, short-lived as it were.

The other thing about the daydreaming situations is that, although all of the bad thoughts started sometime after my dad died when I was 11, I believe the daydreams predated that age. I got that idea from my big sister Barb, who remembers hearing me through the bathroom door talking to myself when I was a child. I don't remember that far back, but if I was talking to myself when I was young, it's a good bet I was having daydreaming sessions in the bathroom (about the only place I could be alone in a house full of eight people).

Finally, I had to admit that the whole daydreaming thing, rather than being anxiety provoking, was actually quite calming. I enjoyed doing it, rather than hated it. For sure, I enjoyed daydreaming a whole lot more than having my head filled with sick, vile thoughts.

I included the daydreaming sessions on my list of obsessions and compulsions simply because it was an odd set of thoughts I had over most of my life. I really had no idea if it fit. The more I thought about it, the less likely it was OCD.

I left the daydreaming sessions on my list simply because I didn't know what else to do with them. I found it dubious they had anything to do with OCD.

I wouldn't find out for a while that I was right.

As I went through ERP therapy, I continued to learn more about OCD. It helped me a lot. The more I learned about the disorder the more I was able to relate it to my own situation.

One thing I learned is that some researchers believe the disorder has a genetic component to it. I could relate to that. In my family, counting myself, my siblings and my nieces and nephews, there are 15 people. At last count, eight of us exhibit signs of the disorder. That's better than 50 per cent of us that have the disorder.

Several people in my family have Tourette's syndrome, which is typified by uncontrollable tics and vocalizations. Still others have one of several different anxiety disorders.

We're one anxious family.

After a couple of sessions of ERP therapy, I became comfortable talking about my OCD, my obsessions and compulsions, in a group setting. I didn't have anything to lose. I was determined to meet the disorder head on and openly participating in the group seemed the right thing to do.

The biggest problem I had with group therapy was that, unlike the three other sufferers, I responded phenomenally well to medications. My obsessions were not bothering me like they used to. I simply wasn't having the same number of obsessions and what was left was weaker and less threatening.

Still, I stuck with ERP therapy because I wanted to learn it. I didn't know if medications would continue to produce great results. I had a genuine fear that the meds would stop working and I'd be faced with dealing with my obsessions on my own. I wanted to be prepared for that eventuality. Twenty per cent of my obsessions were still getting through and I wanted to know ERP well so I could deal with them effectively.

By the end of October and well into ERP therapy, I was beginning to come to grips with the obsessions that had plagued me. Even though I responded very well to medications, I had obsessions popping up in my head on a regular basis. They weren't as strong as they were pre-meds but they still showed up and they still bothered me to some degree.

My reaction to the obsessions was mostly to want to ruminate over them. Ruminating seemed to be the big compulsion I performed whenever obsessions reigned. What I learned in therapy was that I had to let go of the desire to do compulsions and just let the thoughts be.

It's not easy. If a violent, sexual, sick thought pops up in your head, the least you are going to do is react to it. I had spent nearly 40 years reacting to the thoughts I had and it wasn't easy to sit there and do nothing when the thoughts came on. I had to trust in the therapy that leaving the thoughts alone was the right thing to do.

Kids used to be a big trigger for me. Seeing a kid could bring on sexual or violent thoughts and that still happened from time to time, even though I responded so well to meds. When a bad thought about a kid would pop up in my head, I had to do nothing about it. At first, I started to recognize that I was having an intrusive thought. Then I began to tell myself, *it's just a thought*, and then work hard to leave it alone. Sometimes I would recognize an intrusive thought and think to myself, *I'm not going to deal with this thought right now*.

Refocusing became part of my recovery from intrusive thoughts. Those thoughts could show themselves at any time of the day. After recognizing the thought as an intrusive thought and thinking *it's just a thought*, or something similar, I would purposefully try to shift my thinking onto something else. Usually I'd try to refocus onto whatever I was doing at the time. If I were sitting in the Oasis enjoying the day, I'd shift my focus onto looking at the scene around me, noticing the scenery, perhaps studiously watching an eagle in the sky – anything to take my mind off the possibility of ruminating.

At first, I sucked at dealing with nasty thoughts. Things didn't seem to be working out very well. They were telling me in therapy it was the right thing to do and I was determined to figure out how to properly deal with my disorder so I kept trying. Repetition and practice was important because over time it started to work. I would recognize the thought, think *it's just a thought*, or *I'm not going to deal with that thought right now*, and then refocus onto something else. Over time, it got easier and it started working better.

I had to go through a cognitive shift as I dealt with my OCD. I learned in therapy that the disorder isn't just about the intrusive thoughts; it's also about the way sufferers react to the thoughts. Sufferers give too much attention and importance to intrusive thoughts. I started telling myself, *I'm not going to freak out when I get these thoughts anymore.* I had to tell myself that the thoughts were not me, that they were being thrust upon me. I could choose to ignore them, to give them no relevance.

Outside the wonderful job medications had done for me, for the first time in my life I was getting a handle on my

OCD.

I was not yet convinced that all my bad thoughts were caused by a mental disorder called OCD. I felt like they had to come from some other kind of disorder. The thoughts went against who I was as a person but they kept showing up. I didn't know what kind of disorder it could possibly be. Something was causing me to have nasty thoughts about hurting people and awful sexual thoughts that many times included kids. Part of me still felt like I was a sick, twisted bastard for having those morbid thoughts.

While I wrestled with my thoughts and the concept of OCD, life went on in Peachland. No one knew what had happened on the Day from Hell. No one knew I was diagnosed with a mental disorder. No one knew I was in therapy, on medications and working hard to deal with a mental disorder.

We kept it all a secret.

Jackie and I didn't know how to broach the subject. How do you tell your friends, people outside your immediate circle of family members, that you're in the middle of a child pornography investigation? We didn't tell anyone what was going on or about the upheaval our lives had been through since June. We continued on.

My mood continued to improve. For the most part, I was relaxed and calm. I was a little edgy, simply because I had not heard one word from the police or anyone else about what was happening with the legal side of my situation.

In the mean time, I worked hard to beat the disorder I recently learned I had suffered from for nearly four decades.

Chapter 10
Awakenings

If there was one, non-medicinal, non-therapeutic thing I was able to do that made me a feel a little better it was visiting online OCD forums on the web.

I stopped trying to find another person who was exactly like me. With what I had learned about the disorder, I realized sufferers have different obsessions and combinations of obsessions. The likelihood of finding someone exactly like me was remote. I didn't bother.

What I did do was begin to read other people's stories from the lens of learning about OCD. Along the way, I did find people here and there who had some of the same thoughts as me, though no one with the same mix. I wasn't comfortable with posting on forums online. Instead, I went to websites and read the posts from other people. I learned.

There were people who had to arrange things in certain

orders, like me at times. Those people tended to have it far worse than I ever had but I could empathize with what they were experiencing. Many people had harm-thoughts. No one had exactly the same harm-thoughts (what I used to call hurt-thoughts) but I recognized the commonalities.

Reading posts on online forums, I started to pick out the obsessions that caused overwhelming distress for the posters. I picked out the compulsions they were performing to counteract the distress brought on by the obsessions. I saw where other people were having problems, how OCD was affecting their lives and, in the midst of it all, I could relate that back to me. I was beginning to see my obsessions as intrusive, unwanted thoughts that were beyond my control. I began to see my compulsions as behaviour I automatically did but that I had some measure of control over.

More than anything else what the online forums taught me was that I was not alone. Other people out there had the same terrifying thoughts as me. There were many people out there using forums as an outlet for their grief. I started to feel I was part of a community of sufferers, not some guy who was alone with his bad thoughts.

I even found people who had thoughts about sex, and children and sex. I was astounded at the sheer number of people who were posting about having the same kind of thoughts I had since high school. I spent 11 years roaming the Internet, looking for people with the same kind of thoughts as me but rarely found anyone even close. Suddenly I was finding other people like me all over the place.

It gave me some solace to think that there were other people suffering from the same pedophilia thoughts as me.

It troubled me that I couldn't find anyone who had chatted on the Internet about it, been caught and ended up in a legal mess. The more I searched, the more I realized I was unique in that regard. That didn't bode well in my mind. It was a sign that, although I had many similar thoughts to other people, OCD might not be the root cause for my pedophile thoughts. I might be a pedophile and my psychiatrist had it wrong.

I learned a lot from Exposure and Response Prevention (ERP) therapy. It was one of the most valuable types of learning I experienced. I was thankful that the instructors were as open, honest and caring as they were.

The course lasted nine weeks. I learned a lot about the disorder and was exposed, for the first time in my life, to other people who suffered like me. I can't ever talk about what those people said in therapy because we all agreed on day one that what goes on in therapy stays in therapy. I can say that the other people in therapy had vastly different symptoms than I. It was not only my first experience interacting with other sufferers but also my first real experience hearing about other forms of the disorder.

For New Years Jackie, Aaron and I went to Lethbridge to see my sister Barb and her husband Rick. We were met by my sister Janet and her family. All together, there were 11 of us and it was great to spend some stress free time with family in familiar surroundings.

For the next few months, I researched OCD more and more. I checked out online forums to see what people were posting and more importantly, how people were answering other people's posts.

During my 11-year, fruitless effort to prove or disprove

the existence of OCD in my life, I learned that what I probably had, if I had the disorder at all, is something called Pure O. There's a lot of talk on Internet forums about Pure O. There's also a lot of misinformation out there about that subtype of the disorder. It took me a while to figure out exactly what it was and that it was indeed the type of OCD I had.

Pure O stands for Pure Obsession and it's a complete misnomer. Many people think it as a type of Obsessive Compulsive Disorder that is lacking in compulsions.

I knew in my own quest to understand my disorder that although I didn't have outward compulsions that could be seen by others, I had internal, compulsive thought processes.

I researched Pure O a lot on the web. I came to understand it as a type of the disorder where the compulsions are mostly internal, rather than external. You can see a person washing his hands for the thirtieth time that day, but you can't see a person ruminate for hours on end.

I won't say I became obsessed about learning all about OCD, but I was highly motivated to do so. My local library became a great source for information. I took out a number of books on the subject, including 'Brain Lock: Free yourself from Obsessive-Compulsive Behaviour', 'The Boy Who Couldn't Stop Washing' and Howie Mandel's autobiography, 'Here's the Deal: Don't Touch Me'.

Mandel's book was touching for his unrestrained description of his life spent with contamination OCD. Despite having what is likely a severe case, Mandel has been a runaway comedic success. Reading his book showed me that, despite having the disorder, people can do remarkable things.

OCD is a disorder, not a death sentence.

Besides verbal communication with my family members, I barely communicated for months after the cops showed up at my door. I sent a few text messages and talked to family members, but not much else. I stayed off social media. I stayed away from posting on Internet forums. And I didn't write.

Eventually I did something I had done consistently for 10 years but hadn't touched since the Day from Hell. I wrote. One day I sat down at our old clunker of a desktop computer and I wrote the first instalment in a personal journal. The entry described what I had figured out about my daydreaming.

Wednesday, April 9, 2014

Today is the first day I've felt like actually sitting down and starting to write about my experience over the past 10 months. It's going to take a long time to catch up. I'll have to do it piece by piece.

Today was a unique and surprising day for me, having self-diagnosed myself with an officially non-existent disorder. If that sounds confusing, so does the definition of the disorder.

Before I get to the disorder, I need to digress a bit. It was about July of 2013 when I was diagnosed with OCD by my psychiatrist. Later, I believe it was starting in early October, I attended an ERP (Exposure and Response Prevention) therapy group in Kelowna.

One of our tasks at group therapy was to list out our obsessions and compulsions on a chart. I took quite some time doing so and eventually came up with a list of about 17 unique obsessions, quite a lot. One that did not fit had to do with my near constant compulsion to sort of daydream about varying events, situations and characters. I originally wrote that something seemed to trigger these in me and I was sort of compelled to play out a plot in my head. Even as I wrote about this particular compulsion, I knew there was something not quite right with it.

For some reason that one line on my list of obsessions and compulsions did not seem to fit with the rest. It was easy for me to see that what I was doing (living out the daydream in my head) was certainly a compulsion rather than an obsession (it didn't cause distress but rather seemed to relieve it) but it didn't fit with the other compulsions I had written on the list.

My compulsions involve ruminating about a particular obsession. I don't have outward compulsions that are picked up by other people, such as washing my hands or having to turn around four times before walking through a door.

The daydreaming comes with something extra. I talk to myself nearly every time I have one of these episodes. It can range from quietly whispering to myself to outright talking aloud. I also exhibit facial expressions that go along with the situation running through my head.

I talked to Jackie about it today and she said she used to hear me talking to myself in the bathroom in our old apartment when we started living together. Barb told me that I used to talk in the bathroom, by myself, when I was very young.

It is exactly these traits of the daydreaming (facial expressions, talking to myself) that make this different from compulsions. While all of my compulsions take place inside my head, this one happens partly in my head and partly outward where people could see the odd behaviour, if they happened to be close. This is what made me think this particular behaviour did not belong on the obsession and compulsion list and, later, that maybe this wasn't OCD at all.

This morning I drove Aaron to an appointment in Kelowna. I waited in the car, as I always do, as his appointments tend to be short. While I was waiting, I decided to check out posts on a forum.

I scrolled down the list of forum topics and one caught my eye. The subject related to Maladaptive Daydreaming. I had no idea what the latter part meant but I clicked on the topic to read about it.

As I read the initial post I started thinking, *it could be me writing this.* What the person was describing was exactly what I go through every time I daydream.

Maladaptive Daydreaming is not a recognized psychological condition. A doctor coined the term in 2002 to describe the behaviour of some of his patients. The similarity to my situation is uncanny.

I read today about MD (Maladaptive Daydreaming). There are general symptoms that describe someone with MD. The person partakes in excessive daydreaming, creating very complex scenes, plots and characters, much like a movie or a novel. The scenes can take hours, weeks or months to play out, being repeated often with varying twists thrown in. MD can end up taking up so much time that it interferes with the person's life. Often various media can trigger an episode.

Many of the traits of MD I read about describe me

perfectly. If I didn't force myself to concentrate on things I really need to do, I would go on for hours and hours, playing out various scenarios in my head.

My MD is easily triggered by movies, books and television shows. I usually end up as a character in the daydream. Sometimes I am the protagonist, the main good guy character, heroic, the light side in a dark world. Other times I am either a minor character or even the narrator, letting another character steal the limelight but, because I am omniscient, I can see all, know all and even know what the characters are thinking/feeling at the time.

My daydreams usually have a positive outcome, even if the plot seems bleak. There is some kind of redeeming quality to the story.

Some people find MD to be comforting. Others are deeply disturbed by the content of their daydreaming. I think MD was to me a break from the OCD thoughts, a coping mechanism.

I have to say that this MD discovery actually gave me hope. It resolved the lingering doubt I had about daydreaming being a compulsion (which it seems clear it is not).

After writing in my journal, I returned to the Oasis and thought about a pressing issue. Something that bothered me relentlessly going back to the end of July was something my psychiatrist told me.

He said, "It's all OCD." Even the chatting on the Internet was OCD. I had pointedly asked him how the chatting could possibly have anything to do with the disorder. He told me it was possible for someone to become fixated on his or her obsessions.

My psychiatrist's explanation still bothered me. I was a

little anxious every time I thought about it. I thought about it often.

I couldn't connect chatting on the Internet with a disorder that has to do with obsessions and compulsions. I knew that obsessions come from the mind; they are intrusive, unwanted thoughts that cause distress. Chatting on the Internet could not be an obsession. Could it then be a compulsion?

I wrestled with the compulsion possibility. Compulsions are thoughts, acts or behaviours done to counteract obsessions. My obsessions about kids and sex were my most troubling obsessions. They caused the most anxiety. They disturbed me the most.

My psychiatrist was adamant that sufferers could become fixated on their obsessions. It still didn't make sense.

I spent time searching the Internet for some kind of further explanation about this incongruous situation. I even Googled the words 'OCD' and 'fixate'. All the searching and thinking about it did nothing but put me into a further state of consternation. It was starting to drive me nuts.

Maybe I needed to see my psychiatrist. Because my medications had been tweaked to the right cocktail, my symptoms were reduced by an impressive 80 per cent or better and I had undergone ERP therapy, there wasn't any reason to see my psychiatrist any more so we had parted company.

It wasn't like I could set another appointment, go in, and have a chat with him. I discovered I would have to start over and go and see my GP, get a referral to Kelowna Mental Health, and then I might get in to see my old psychiatrist. I was frustrated.

I had the answer. I had become fixated on my obsessions. However, I wanted a better answer. What I wanted was for my psychiatrist to tell me it was still all OCD and that the chatting did indeed have to do with OCD.

I figured out what this need to know meant only after I began spending some time with other people with Obsessive Compulsive Disorder.

In my travels around the Internet, I found an OCD forum run by OCD-UK. I began visiting it regularly. Although it was based in the United Kingdom and primarily dealt with people from the UK, there were people from all over the world that posted on the forum. It was open to anyone. What struck me about that forum was that it was very active, with lots of posts every day and there was a general feeling of compassion and understanding between the users.

I told Jackie I wanted to sign up at the forum. She was hesitant about my getting involved with an online community. She was concerned that the police were monitoring our Internet usage. I was tired of being a castaway in my own backyard and I was truly interested in interacting with other sufferers.

I made my first post on the OCD-UK forum. Every day after, usually more than once, I would check the forum for new posts and add my two cents. I was careful in the beginning to read more and post less. I learned as I posted and I posted more as I learned. What I ended up signing up for was a forum populated entirely by sufferers who offered advice and a shoulder to lean on.

Posting on the forum empowered me. I told part of my story but I steered clear of talking about the child pornography charges.

I noticed on the forum there were people of all types seeking help and giving assistance. There were men and women posting, from teenagers to retirees, representing a wide range of themes and severity. There were people posting who had recently discovered they had OCD and others who had known for decades. Every stage of the path to wellness was represented on the forum.

There were a few people offering assistance who had been able to get rid of their symptoms. Other helpers were at a stage like me, mostly recovered and able to control their obsessions through strategies learned in therapy.

Medication was a hot topic on the forum. There were strong proponents of meds for mental disorders and others who were dead set against them. When it came to medication, it became abundantly clear that not everyone had as positive a reaction as I did.

The forum espoused the usefulness of Cognitive Behavioural Therapy and Exposure and Response Prevention – the same therapies I learned in group therapy.

Day in and day out, I read posts on the forum and responded as best I could. I was far from an expert but I felt very comfortable communicating with other sufferers.

There were people with contamination obsessions, some who had to touch, count or arrange things and still others who relentlessly checked that doors were closed and locks were locked. Many of the people on the forum had Pure O type obsessions -- they all had internal compulsions.

Soon after becoming a member of the OCD-UK forum, I realized that many of the sufferers posting were seeking reassurance.

When I was in group therapy for OCD, the instructors

were very careful not to offer reassurance to the sufferers in the group. They explained that "reassurance seeking" is a form of compulsion that only leads to more reassurance seeking. A few times at group therapy, one of the instructors refused to answer a question from a sufferer in the group because it could have been construed as offering reassurance. On the forum, reassurance seeking was almost a sport. It wasn't the fault of the users; they either didn't know they were doing it or simply couldn't help themselves.

Repeatedly I saw a user (usually a newer one) asking for some kind of reassurance. Someone asked in a post if it's okay to have shoes in the house from outside or is it better to leave them outside the front door because they might be contaminated with dog poop. People asked if they're a pedophile or not, asked what they should do if their clothing touches the toilet or tried to pin down the probability they will stab their partner with a knife in the kitchen.

Reassurance seeking is a compulsion. It does no good. In the short term, reassurance makes the sufferer feel better. The feeling is short lived. Then whatever obsession triggered the event starts up again and the sufferer is compelled to ask for more reassurance.

It is hard not to give reassurance, especially when it is obvious the person making the request is terrified. It is so easy to post reassuring words, knowing it might have a positive effect. But it's the wrong thing to do because the positive effect will quickly end. The sufferer will be caught in a cycle of constantly asking for more reassurance.

Compounding the problem of reassurance seeking is sufferers who seek reassurance over the problem of whether they have OCD or not. They think maybe they are capable of performing whatever the obsession is about (like stabbing someone with a knife) and they seek reassurance that the disorder is the cause of the thoughts.

We tried to explain that reassurance seeking itself is a known and very prevalent compulsion. In addition, the person always has some kind of intrusive thought (obsession) that causes distress. Add up obsessions and compulsions and you have OCD.

We also tried to explain to sufferers that reassurance seeking is a compulsion and does no good. In fact, they help to reinforce obsessions. The reassurance seeking needs to be resisted and eventually stopped.

Another major issue I really learned about on the forum was that of the search for certainty. Certainty and OCD do not mix. Why would someone check the lock on the door after locking the door? They're not certain. Why does someone wash their hands three times in a row? They're not certain they're clean. Why does the thought of pushing someone in front of a bus cause such grief? Because the sufferer isn't certain they won't do it.

I saw many examples on the forum of people searching for certainty. There are people who are wracked with guilt because they cannot be certain they love their significant other. There are people who are completely frustrated because they aren't sure they have the disorder. There are people who aren't sure they won't push someone down a set of stairs or poke the eye of a random person on the street.

OCD is a state of mind where certainty and assurance are sought but rarely accepted as truth.

And then it dawned on me.

It was suddenly so clear. I had not achieved a sufficient level of certainty over the issue of chatting on the Internet being OCD. I also had a very strong urge to seek reassurance from my psychiatrist. I was acting like other sufferers on the forum.

I realized I was seeking both certainty and reassurance over whether the pedophile thoughts and chatting on the Internet was OCD. It was suddenly so clear to me. I had to accept that the pedophile thoughts were obsessions and the chatting was a compulsion.

OCD is a weird disorder. It can latch onto almost anything and make a huge problem out of it. After spending more than three decades believing I was an evil person for my horrendous thoughts, I had a hard time accepting all of my psychiatrist's diagnosis. My disorder latched onto that and soon enough I was looking for certainty and wanting to perform a compulsion by contacting my psychiatrist for reassurance.

Once I figured it out, I implemented the same strategy I told users of the forum to follow. When I got the urge to call my psychiatrist to discuss things further, I labelled it for what it was, the desire to perform a compulsion. I told myself I would not seek reassurance over the matter. I continued with my day, accepting the anxiety the situation created, knowing that anxiety could not hurt me.

It took months for me to let go my need for reassuring. As I let go the urge to be reassured, I began to gain confidence that my problem, my whole problem, was related to OCD. I slowly began to understand that all my bad thoughts were obsessions and chatting on the Internet was something I did because I was fixated on some of the bad thoughts I had, just like my psychiatrist said.

Chapter 11
Working At It

My sister Barb and my wife Jackie broached the subject that something good had to come out of everything I had gone through and that I was going to go through. They were quick to point out that the biggest good thing had already happened – I was diagnosed with OCD and was getting better.

The other good thing, they said, was maybe there might be a book in me about my journey. Jackie looked at the idea of a book as a way to stand up for myself and for those with Obsessive Compulsive Disorder.

I had to admit the idea both intrigued and scared me. On one hand, my story might be interesting enough for a book. There's suffering for 40 years with a mental disorder, getting in trouble with the law, being diagnosed, receiving treatment, getting better. That sounds interesting. On the other hand, the subject matter is troubling to say the least. It would be a touchy subject to put down on paper.

One thing I continually practiced was ERP. I was taught Exposure and Response Prevention at the course I took in the fall and I definitely needed to put it into practice.

Although medications alone reduced my intrusive thoughts and the time I spent on compulsions by about 80 per cent, I still had 20 per cent of the thoughts getting through. With the sheer number of intrusive thoughts I used to get, 20 per cent was still a significant number.

I began putting ERP into practice with my obsession about not locking the car door when I went somewhere. I purposefully exposed myself to that which caused me anxiety (parking somewhere, locking the door and walking away) and worked to stop compulsions (caving in and relocking the car). Once I had successfully put that particular obsession in its place, my attention turned to other obsessions that were still coming through.

Implementing ERP for many of my obsessions was not easy because I have mostly Pure O varieties of the disorder and they don't come with physical compulsions to stop. Instead, the compulsions are mental in origin, chief among them ruminating. Ruminating is nothing more than thinking hard and ERP taught me that I had to stop ruminating, which in effect means stop thinking. It's not an easy to thing to stop thinking about something.

Occasionally the old obsession of seeing me drive into the front of a gravel truck made itself known. At those times, I tried to let the thought pop up in my head and I worked hard not to go over the thought in my head. I just left the thought alone.

I went a step further and, as I drove, I purposefully triggered myself when I saw a gravel truck by thinking, *I'm going to drive into the front end of that truck.* Then I would make sure I didn't do any compulsions in my head. It took time but, like the car locking obsession, this obsession soon lessened and ceased to become a problem.

One type of obsession that was still going through my head, although they were less intense because of the meds, was the intrusive thoughts about sex and children. They were the most deeply rooted obsessions. They were something I suffered from for about 35 years and I guess it made sense they weren't going to easily leave my mind.

For pedophile thoughts, I followed what I had done for the car locking thoughts and the gravel truck thoughts. I purposefully exposed myself to thoughts of sex and children in my mind and then worked not to perform any compulsions. I let the thoughts rattle around in my mind without reacting to them. It wasn't easy. A part of me wanted desperately to analyze the thoughts and try to figure out if they were true or real.

If pedophile thoughts popped into my head on their own, I thought to myself, *that's an OCD thought*, then shifted my focus to something else (usually whatever I was doing at the time, like washing the dishes or reading a book) while being cognizant of compulsions and making sure I didn't perform them.

It took months of exposures and not performing compulsions for the pedophile thoughts to decrease. They decreased in both quantity and duration. Eventually they became wisps of the thoughts without power over me. They were sad little thoughts that became easier and easier to dismiss, like flicking a bug off my arm with a finger.

Chapter 12
A little OCD

I was diagnosed with OCD. When I completed the Y-BOCS checklist, I discovered I had suffered for nearly four decades from a severe to extreme case of the disorder. I became invested in my recovery. I took medications. I learned about the disorder and learned some more. Over time, the fundamentals and treatment of OCD became present in my mind.

A considerable amount of my time was invested in the disorder. I Google searched OCD and related terms. I read many blogs written by sufferers. I read research papers. I wanted to know what sufferers were talking about so I scoured forums. I even saw posts on Twitter and Facebook.

And I saw the jokes.

Did you know you could tell the school kid with OCD because his crayons are all perfectly aligned on his desk?

That's not true but people don't let the truth get in the way of what they think is funny.

The Internet is replete with OCD jokes. An image search on Google led me to discover the OCD clock. Instead of 12 hours, there are 12 messages. One o'clock says wash your hands. Five o'clock is check stove. Nine o'clock has some other message. None of it is particularly true and it's certainly not something I found funny.

Most people don't have a clue what OCD is. They don't treat it like the devastating disorder it can be. They mock it. To them OCD is not a disorder. It's a personality quibble, a sign of someone slightly off. People don't suffer. They have odd quirks.

Somewhere along the way, OCD became the quirky little brother to the mental illness family. It became a joke. Somehow, some way, Obsessive Compulsive Disorder was relegated to the pile of Odd Things People Do. It even became in vogue to emulate the disorder and claim it as one's own. Anal retentive became synonymous with OCD. Neat and clean were attributes of OCD, claimed by many.

Then there's the saying that is spoken by many, "I'm a little OCD." A woman spends a couple of hours straightening out her junk drawer and suddenly she's a little OCD today.

I saw comments by the dozen on Twitter from people claiming to have OCD because they straightened something up or cleaned something. I discovered my life had been marred by a devastating mental disorder and then I saw examples of people cheapening my pain by making other people think the disorder I have is about being a neat fusspot.

To muddy the waters further, many people don't just

claim the disorder as their own; they claim they are the disorder. I don't know how many times I saw people use social media to claim they are OCD. Someone would write, "I'm so OCD today." What is that? Where does that come from? No one says, "I'm so cancer today," or "I feel so liver disease right now". Yet it seems perfectly normal for people to claim they are OCD.

If you don't have OCD then you don't have OCD. It's not something you catch like a wave of energy, ride it out, clean like mad then settle back down into a non-OCD state. No such thing. You don't get temporary fits of the disorder, like you're sitting at a desk and suddenly you organize your paperclips and you sit back and exclaim, "Well that was a little OCD!"

When people experience a cleaning or straightening up fit, they want to do it. They want to put their heart and soul into the project and stand back at the end feeling they've accomplished something worthwhile. That doesn't make them have OCD. People with the disorder don't want to do their compulsions. They loathe their compulsions. If cleaning and organizing were compulsions of a sufferer, the last thing the sufferer would want is to clean and organize. He'd do it anyway because he felt compelled to do so.

You aren't clinically depressed because you had a sad day. You aren't bipolar just because you had a good morning and a bad afternoon. If you have the creepy sensation someone is watching you it doesn't make you a paranoid schizophrenic. If the boss made you wait outside his office before tearing you a new asshole, that doesn't qualify you as having an anxiety disorder. And you don't have OCD unless you do. If you do and you know you do, then you know it's the last thing you want anyone to make a joke over.

OCD is no joke. It's a serious mental disorder that at best is a real pain in the ass and at worst is so debilitating as to preclude any kind of normal life. It can rip apart friendships and relationships, confine people to their homes or one room, sap the life out of sufferers and drive some to contemplate suicide.

OCD is where all the world's worst fears reside. It's a place of excruciating anxiety, severe doubt and manic dread. People with the disorder can find relationships painful. Many don't last. Days of work are missed. Work can be impossible. Concentration is a thing heard about but rarely practiced by the sufferer. Life is inexorably altered, for the negative.

People without OCD who claim they have it do so out of ignorance. They don't understand the disorder. They hear of someone else making an ignorant claim of being stricken with the disorder and they mimic what they heard, repeat it and spread the ignorance. They don't know they're making a mistake by representing the disorder as a fixation on being neat and clean. Most people aren't being mean when they misrepresent OCD; they just don't know any better.

As I was helping people on the OCD-UK forum, I came up with a different way to describe what goes on in the brains of sufferers. It was sort of a layperson's description of the disorder.

In every person's brain, there is a sentry. It takes all the information coming into the brain, or generated by the brain itself, and it decides what to do with the information. The sentry decides that a thought is worth remembering, worth acting on immediately or not worth keeping. In people with OCD, the sentry does not work properly.

In a person without OCD, the thought *I should jump off this tall building* is discarded with little effort. The thought is shifted to the brain's trash bin. In a person with the disorder, the thought is treated as real. It triggers the brain's automatic fight or flight response. Anxiety levels increase. The person feels terribly uncomfortable and responds by doing some kind of compulsion, perhaps stepping back and getting to someplace safe.

There is no triggering of the fight or flight response in people about to clean out their junk drawer. Anxiety levels don't increase for people who are about to spend four hours expertly cleaning their apartment.

OCD sufferers have genuine feelings of panic. There can be a physical, unpleasant response to the thought. The thought, as silly as it is to the non-sufferer, is real to the sufferer.

Without the proper therapy, there is no cognitive learning with OCD. The next time such a thought appears in the brain, the sentry treats it as a real, pressing concern. In an OCD brain, the thoughts (obsessions) can come relentlessly and each time the sentry treats the thought as real, filling the sufferer with alarm.

Compulsions, which are performed to alleviate the distress caused by the thoughts, are a natural response. Obsessions in a sense cause pain; compulsions try to minimize the pain.

It seems there are as many themes as there are types of flowers we could plant in the Oasis. The general public has almost no idea these themes even exist.

I figured out that the average person believes people with OCD either wash their hands a lot or organize their pens and pencils with precision.

Part of the problem is that sufferers in general are loathe to talk about their obsessions and the more bizarre, twisted or evil the thoughts are, the less likely a person is to talk about them. Who would want to tell a loved one or friend that they believe they killed someone while drunk last Saturday night? How many people would talk to others at a cocktail party about how they have thoughts all the time about stabbing people with knives or pushing people in front of trains? Who goes on daytime talk shows to tell the world they are constantly bombarded with thoughts of child sexual abuse?

As sufferers, we instinctively try to protect ourselves. We hide behind a wall of shame. We chastise ourselves for having the thoughts in the first place (even though it's not our fault). We dread the idea of sharing our innermost, awful thoughts with others. Except on Internet forums, in therapist offices or at support groups, we don't talk about our thoughts. We keep them hidden from others and in doing so we keep them hidden from the world.

We aren't about to openly share our obsessions and that means the world stays ignorant to our plight. We suffer terribly from our thoughts and our incessant need to perform compulsions, yet we suffer alone. We wish other people could understand but we are terrified of explaining.

Because of our silence, the world has only a basic, very limited understanding of the depths of our despair. And it is despair. Not only do we suffer but also we know that we are suffering. We know there is something inherently not right with our conditions. We don't share and the world believes only what it is told and it isn't told much.

Chapter 13
Everything Happens For A Reason

Jackie is a big believer in the saying, everything happens for a reason. She's said it a million times in the 30 years we've been together. I wasn't always the type of person to buy into it but I started thinking differently.

I watched a show on TV that really stuck with me. The show was about how to succeed in this world, how to pick yourself up when you've fallen down. One of the guests on the show was an NFL football player who went astray and ended up doing something not good. His career and life suffered.

The host of the show looked at the former football player and said the same thing Jackie said so many times. Everything happens for a reason. It was up to the man to figure out what lesson he was to learn from the hardship he had created.

That moment struck me and stuck with me. What's my lesson? I went from the Day from Hell when the cops came to my house to months of worry. I learned I had OCD. I realized that I suffered from OCD. I started to get better. Where's the lesson in that?

I suffered from Obsessive Compulsive Disorder for 40 years. I didn't tell a soul. I kept it a secret. Not only did the disorder torture me for four decades, I tortured myself by constantly saying that I was a bad, evil, mean person for the thoughts inside my head. I suffered in more than one way.

Had I taken a leap of faith and told someone I had raging, awful, uncontrollable thoughts, I might have received the help I needed and everything in my life would have changed. I'm not sure I would have learned a lesson, however.

No, I had to screw up in a big way, thanks to OCD's help, to be put into a position where the lesson could be realized. Somewhere in the midst of the stress, anxiety and hopelessness, was a lesson to learn.

I should have been in my darkest moment. Instead, I was instead uplifted and calm. Where there should have been despair I found hope.

I had every reason to hate myself for such a long time. I truly believed the thoughts were a part of me, that they were me. With that belief in mind, I found little about me to like and little less to love. There were times in my life when I complained, even openly, that all my time and effort was being spent on making other people money or somehow making life better for other people. What was missing was some kind of monetary or other kind of reward for me.

It became clear: the reason I was putting other people first was that I was putting myself dead last. It was all by design. OCD made me feel terrible. I felt terrible about myself. I was a second-class citizen in my eyes. No matter the achievements I racked up in my life, I felt I wasn't worthy. It was all done on purpose, though. I put myself in the position of being below other people. I believed I was a bad person and I treated myself like a bad person.

Once I was diagnosed, I chose to be well and worked hard to get there. My mind cleared of the horrible thoughts. My mood swung from depression to a happier state. I liked waking up in the morning to see what the day would bring. I wasn't anxious all the time. Stress came but bled off as it had never done before. I began to treat other people more honestly and openly. Above all else, I began to right a wrong that had begun when I was 11. I began to like myself.

That was the lesson for me.

That's why I had to go through all the stress and heartache starting the day the police showed up at my door. For 40 years, I did not take care of myself. I didn't take care of my physical, emotional, psychological or spiritual needs. I didn't think I was worth it. I needed an epic shock to my system to show me it was time to take care of me.

I'm worth it. I'm worth taking care of. I'm worth nurturing. I'm worth the peace I've found through medications, therapy and personal growth. I'm special, unique, awesome, and wonderful. Like it says in my favourite poem, The Desiderata: "You are a child of the universe, no less than the trees and the stars. You have a right to be here."

<> <> <>

Overall, things weren't bugging me as they used to. Negative situations simply didn't have the control over me as they had through most of my life. I was able to take in the negativity, realize I had little control over its existence and get on with my life with little interruption. It was a wholly new way of experiencing life for me. I liked it. I liked it a lot.

When I was 10, I was a free spirit. Life was good. I had friends, a family, a vivid imagination, lots of free time, a healthy collection of stuffed animals and a sparkle in my eye. When I was 11, my world fell apart. My dad died on a frozen Alberta highway. What I now know as OCD grabbed hold of me.

For the next close to 40 years, I was consumed by raging thoughts that profoundly affected my life and how I lived. I may have been on the highway of life but the disorder was in the driver's seat. Whatever I did, I did well, but I rarely felt that what I was doing was what I was supposed to be doing. Something was missing. I worked in retail most of my life but it was unsatisfying. I was in management from my early 20s until my late 30s. It wasn't what I wanted.

I had a hole in my soul that OCD dug out and I was unable to fill it. I was living but I wasn't living with purpose. Writing was the closest I came to filling the void. I loved communicating. I loved telling people things they didn't know. But there was always something missing. It was as if I was close to being who I was supposed to be but not quite there yet. I wasn't in sync with my soul.

Everything happens for a reason.

Jackie told me something that stuck with me. She didn't

like me not working any more than I did, but she looked at the time I was off work as a time of healing. After suffering for 40 years, I needed some time to put myself together, to heal from a life spent with a terrible mental disorder.

OCD is poorly understood. It is so misunderstood that people regularly make jokes about it, not understanding they unintentionally belittle the suffering of people with the disorder. I reached a point where I wanted to change that.

Not working meant I had plenty of time to think. What I was thinking was that everything that had happened before, everything I had experienced, both good and bad, was all for a reason. The world can always use more understanding. If there's one thing I had a lot of experience with, it is living with OCD. Who better, my thinking went, to help people understand the disorder than a sufferer of it?

People suffering from OCD, especially if the theme is based on morbid obsessions like harm, sex or pedophilia, are loathe talking about their thoughts. That serves only to keep the problem hidden. In my case, the cat was truly out of the bag. OCD, more specifically my poor handling of the disorder, had forced me to rock bottom. Telling my story and thus educating people about the dark side of the disorder could not hurt me more. In fact, I believed that talking about that which is not openly discussed would be freeing.

I used to feel jealous of people who seemed to have their shit together and they were doing what they were supposed to be doing. I used to marvel at people who found, long into their lives, their special purpose. I reached a point where I marvelled over how I found my purpose, my special talent, the way to fill the hole in my soul.

I began to write my book.

Chapter 14
A forgiving season

The winter of 2014/2015 was reasonably mild in the Okanagan Valley compared to the rest of Canada. The East was pummelled by one snowstorm after another for what seemed like months, with record setting chilly temperatures in places like Toronto. Meanwhile, back in Peachland, we had one near record dump of snow and then mild temperatures for the rest of the winter.

Winter was so mild that things started sprouting up out of the ground about a month earlier than normal. By the middle of February, crocuses were pushing through the soil in the front of our house and our one chive plant in the back yard was two inches high by the end of the month.

I spent a good chunk of the winter going through the motions, working on my book, waiting and thinking. It slowly dawned on me that I was in one weird position.

If I were to be charged with a crime or crimes based on chatting on the Internet, then my legal case could involve the fact I had OCD. In fact, the disorder could be part of my defense. Surely the majority of people out there, if they heard such a thing, would think it absurd, or worse.

People have preconceived notions about things and OCD is no exception. The general public walks around all day with the belief that the disorder involves anal retentive neat freaks who do weird rituals. But, as I discovered, there are the Pure O varieties that most people have never heard of. There are women who feel tremendous guilt over something as simple as a glance at a good-looking man. Some men are bombarded by images of homosexual sex. There are gay people who are abused by thoughts they might be straight. People have harm images of the vilest variety. There are thoughts of stabbing, mutilating, raping, and killing. And some people have thoughts of being a pedophile.

People have strong feelings about pedophiles. They are looked upon with hate, contempt, disdain and they are ostracized by whole communities. Perhaps rightfully so. But what would an average person think if they were told that there are people who suffer from a form of OCD that involves intrusive thoughts of a pedophilia nature? I surmise the average person would equate people with such thoughts as being no different from pedophiles.

Indeed, a search on the Internet will not net anyone a whole bunch of stories similar to mine where people chatted on chat rooms, got into legal trouble, and discovered it was all because of Obsessive Compulsive Disorder. I for one spent hundreds of hours on the OCD-UK forum, amassing thousands of responses of my own, and I did not come across one person exactly like me.

I wasn't worried. Far from far it. Since the day my psychiatrist told me, "It's all OCD," I had learned an awful lot about the disorder and came to know it intimately. I understood that, as bizarre as it sounds, my chatting was a type of compulsion that I felt I had to do to keep my own sanity. Mine is likely one of the only kinds of compulsions there is that can lead a person into a legal mess.

That isn't to say I didn't come close to finding some people who suffered from compulsions that had legal implications. A female member of the forum posted that she had, on several occasions, Googled the search term 'child porn'. She was very distressed that she had done it. She didn't understand why she had done it. She felt alone and vulnerable. Then someone else posted that he too had done the same thing.

The woman who initially posted made it clear that if she found any child pornography in her search that she would report it to the authorities straight away but that doesn't absolve her having searched for the term in the first place. Why in the world would she do that? Why would she do that, given the possibility that child sex images could have been sent over the Internet to her computer and then reside on her computer, making her culpable of an illegal act?

Compulsions. They are motivators that make people with OCD do strange things. A man believes he could have germs on his hands, so he scrubs his hands hard. Soon after he believes the germs are back, so he repeats the compulsion. It's far more complex a situation with pedophile thoughts than it is for the hand washer who scrubs his hands raw every day.

There are legal implications with pedophilia. It is illegal

to possess, distribute or make child sex images and it is illegal to have sex with children. It's not illegal to wash your hands fifty times a day. It's not illegal to spend nine hours thinking about whether you love your spouse or not. It's not illegal to avoid asbestos.

It is not illegal to have murderous thoughts (a type of OCD) but it is illegal to murder someone. It's not illegal to have pedophile thoughts but it is illegal to perform pedophilia. A person with harm OCD, who constantly thinks about stabbing people with knives, might go on the Internet to search images of people being stabbed. OCD sufferers do such things to try to convince themselves they aren't evil. They could also search such images to check what their reaction would be to such images. Checking is a well-known compulsion.

The same is true for pedophile thoughts, only actually finding such images would be illegal. If a person with murderous thoughts can perform a compulsion by looking for images or written words about murder, it holds true that the same type of thing would happen for someone with pedophile thoughts. Only the person with pedophile thoughts risks breaking the law if he does the wrong thing.

In a way, people with OCD with a pedophile theme are doubly screwed. They are first inundated with terrible thoughts or images they can't get rid of. Then they run the risk of breaking the law if they perform the wrong compulsion, like chatting on the Internet.

My case was not terribly different from many others I came across on the forum. All the people with pedophile thoughts either thought they had done something inappropriate or believed they could do something inappropriate (and illegal). On average, they spent almost as much time trying to convince other people on the forum that they were bad people as they did getting help to deal with their thoughts.

In my case, I was inundated with child sex abuse images and thoughts from the time I was about 15 to the time I was 49. For about 34 years, those thoughts invaded my mind every day. I had many other thoughts that came and went but the pedophile thoughts were the worst and the most persistent. Sometime during that more than three decades, I came to believe that, deep down, I was a pedophile.

For 25 years, I had no concept of OCD and pedophile thoughts. For another 10 years, I had a basic understanding of the disorder but little understanding of my thoughts about child sex abuse. Being pummelled with images and thoughts, every day, for three and a half decades, took a big toll on me. I concluded that I was what I thought. I saw it a lot on the forum, where people were convinced they were pedophiles. They couldn't see the difference between themselves and a pedophile.

Which brings me to the ultimate question of the day: what is the difference between a pedophile and a person with pedophilia thoughts?

It's the same thing as the difference between a person with murderous thoughts (in the context of OCD) and a murderer. Many people with the disorder have thoughts about harming other people (all the way up to some sort of murder). What differentiates them from murderers? They don't murder. They don't do anything. There is no intent to harm, no planning of the crime involved.

The same holds true for people with OCD who have pedophilia thoughts. They don't do anything. There is no sexual abuse of children involved. There is no intent. No planning. There is no action.

OCD becomes so nasty that it becomes all encompassing. Sufferers can end up thinking about almost nothing but their obsessions. The same holds true for obsessions involving pedophile thoughts. It certainly did with me. Scores of times every day I got intrusive thoughts about children and sex. For every obsession that popped up, there was corresponding compulsions that needed to be performed. It involved ruminating – thinking about thoughts, repeatedly, going over the thoughts in my head, trying to analyze the thoughts, and on and on. My compulsions evolved to include talking about my thoughts by putting them on a computer screen and talking as if I was what I believed I had become a pedophile.

One compulsion common to those with pedophile thoughts is to actually search on the Internet about pedophiles. They want to learn what pedophiles are, how they act, what they do, who they are. It's all a part of being fixated on the topic, a way of checking to see if there are comparisons between the person with OCD and the real McCoy.

That's what I was doing, in a way, when I chatted on the Internet about a horrible subject. I was performing a compulsion, yes, but I was performing a checking compulsion. Checking is a well-known type of compulsion. By talking about the thoughts I'd had for decades, by acting out those thoughts on a dark Internet chat room, I was in effect checking to see if I was a pedophile. Given my thoughts, I had every reason to believe I was. Yet there was always doubt lingering. By chatting I was trying to prove to myself, one way or the other, that I was or wasn't a pedophile. It sounds strange but there are precedents. There are people who believed themselves to be heterosexual who are so tortured by homosexual thoughts that they will go out and have homosexual sex to try and prove, one way or the other, what they truly are. In the end, it doesn't work. It doesn't solve anything. The intrusive thoughts are relentless, they bother the sufferer greatly and no final answer is achieved. It's a no-win situation and it certainly was no-win in my case.

I concluded, and I'm very confident in it, that one day, when my story gets out, I'll be contacted by a few people at least, who have similar stories to mine. I don't believe I'm the only one. I don't believe I'm the only person whose compulsions got them into trouble.

The worst thing about all of this is that there are people out there suffering and partaking in dangerous compulsions without a clue they have OCD. Maybe my story might change that, at least for some of those people. Maybe if they find my story, it will dawn on them that they aren't psychotic, they aren't crazy and they aren't pedophiles.

I came to know that I wasn't. The day the police showed up at my door, I believed I was the worst scum on earth. I didn't deserve to live. I didn't want to live. Fast forward a few months, I understood the disorder I previously didn't really know I had.

What I did, chatting on the Internet, may not have been right, but I understood that it was all linked to a nasty mental disorder – one that I not only came to understand but that I managed well. No longer was I inundated with terrible thoughts. No longer did I spend hours and hours a day on various compulsions that only made the situation worse. No longer was I fixated.

I went from being in the midst of a devastating disorder to understanding that disorder, to helping people from all over the world to not only understand their version of the disorder but to learn how to live despite having it.

Things changed for me because I was forced into changing. The police showing up at my door started the process. I made the choice to seek help. I educated myself about the disorder. I participated in the right therapy for the disorder. I did the hard work required. I put the concepts into practice.

Eventually I realized that all of my intrusive thoughts were because of OCD and that chatting on the Internet was just another crazy compulsion. I took my psychiatrist's words, "It's all OCD," to heart. I understood the words and I believed the words.

Above all else, I did something I could not have dreamed of when I was lying under that burned out log near the creek on the Day from Hell. I did it without fanfare or announcement. There were no balloons, no cake, and no congratulatory banner to mark the occasion. I did the one thing that would mean more to me than a positive result of my legal case, that even meant more than the support and love I continually received from my family. It came to me slowly, without fanfare and from my heart.

I forgave myself. With that, I became more than my disorder.

Part 3
<> <> <>
Resolution

Chapter 15
Bad News

Five months after the Day from Hell the news we were dreading came in a way I was not expecting.

It was November. Winter's chill hung in the air. The sky threatened snow. The Oasis was empty and stark, awaiting warmer days to become our place of refuge in the back yard.

I was in the kitchen of our small home, cleaning up after supper, when my wife's best friend walked through our back door. She was clearly distraught. She told me straight up she had heard on the evening news that I was being charged with child pornography offences.

My anxiety rose to a level it had not been for five months. My heart sunk in my chest. I went back to that bad place where anxiety was overwhelming. My emotions twisted and turned. My worst fear was being realized. Not only was I being charged with a crime, but also everyone in the world was hearing about it. If it were on one news channel, it would be on every news channel. The newspapers would pick it up.

Since the Day from Hell, I had secluded myself to my home. I went out to stores, did the shopping, saw some people on the street but otherwise stuck to home – a place where I could feel safe with the people that helped me feel safe. No one outside our home, other than a few police officers and a few members of my immediate family, knew the police had shown up with a search warrant, about me going missing for 17 hours, my subsequent diagnosis of OCD and successfully taming that hellish disorder.

With the media blitz, everyone would know the sordid part. My thoughts overwhelmed me. I wanted to escape, to run away again. I couldn't think. My feelings were topsy-turvy. I felt panicked again, short of breath and alone. While my wife's friend went to talk to Jackie, I grabbed the car keys and headed out to the car. I got in and drove. I made it to an isolated parking lot on the south side of town.

"My life is over," I texted to my big sister Barb. She texted me back immediately.

"No it's not. Go home."

I got texts from Jackie and from my son Garrett, who lived with Barb in Lethbridge.

I felt overwhelmed thinking about all the people out there who knew me finding out I was involved in a despicable investigation. Relaxation therapy taught me to breathe through the tough times and that's what I did. About all I could do was breathe. I closed my eyes for a few moments. I breathed as deeply as I could.

I drove back home.

The cat was truly out of the bag. By the time I got home, Jackie had explained the entire situation to her friend. I walked from the car to the Oasis and sat. The full realization of the world knowing about me sank deep onto my shoulders.

I knew almost immediately what had happened, though it seemed incredibly unfair to me. Yes, I was the bad guy the cops were after, but I thought there would have been some kind of decency shown by letting me know first that charges would be laid. That didn't happen.

As an experienced reporter, I knew that in my case the police had sent out a press release that day to the media. I also knew the police hadn't bothered to tell me charges were being laid. It seemed especially cruel to me that the world found out about the charges before I did.

How the hell could the police send out a press release announcing my name and the charges against me without first telling me about the charges? It was like being crucified in the press without any consideration for my feelings or state of mind.

It took months for both Jackie and I to settle down a bit from the unexpected arrival of the police at our door. Now our lives were once again turned upside down, only this time our situation was splashed all over the news.

I couldn't watch the news. I refused to watch the news. I used to be a reporter. I knew the local media knew me and would be chomping at the bit to get the news out quickly. I was the new dastardly flavour of the day and I knew the media was going to jump all over the story and report it everywhere. I was, in a small way, a celebrity in Peachland and the old axiom in journalism was holding true: the bigger they are, the harder they fall.

Suddenly I'm big news. Everyone in town and beyond knows about the charges against me. I live in a small town. I haven't worked for five months. How am I going to get a job? How can I walk into a store and talk about getting a job when my name is all over the news? How can I go to a store to get a jug of milk when my name is now synonymous with something sick and twisted? How will people treat me? Will they see me in public and give me bad looks? Will they walk right up to me and call me a bastard?

The worst part of the situation was that Jackie would take the brunt of the fallout. I could remain at home, spending my time cleaning the house, making meals and sitting thinking in the Oasis, but she had to go out, work and interact with people every day. I could hide. Jackie could not.

Right away, Barb and my son Garrett decided they needed to be in Peachland to support Jackie and me. They left the next day for the long drive from Lethbridge. I was glad Barb and Garrett arrived. It was nice to have some more supporters close to me. I knew Jackie needed the interaction with people who loved us.

One day later, there was a knock on the door just past seven in the morning. The untimely knocking immediately awakened everyone in the house.

It's the cops. It's the cops and they've come to take me away. I'm going to be arrested. They'll put handcuffs on me, they'll take me away, and my family will be standing there watching me walk toward a cop car. That has to be it. It works on TV cop shows that way. I'm screwed.

It was a police officer at the front door. She asked for

me as I came down the stairs. I told her my name and she handed me two pieces of paper stapled together. She explained what was on the papers, that I was to appear in court in December and that I had to appear at the Kelowna RCMP detachment for fingerprinting and to have my mugshot taken on that same day.

Jackie jumped at the chance to ask the female officer why she was bringing the summons two days after it first appeared in the news. The officer surmised that some enterprising media person had discovered information about the court appearance date and was able to put together the story.

I knew that story was bullshit. Many media outlets in the Okanagan Valley announced news of the charges against me. Some reporter didn't pick up the story. The RCMP released the story to the media. Somewhere along the way, wires may have been crossed but I ended up getting officially informed about the charges nearly 48 hours after the first media report.

The officer did mention that they had a call stating I needed to be served with the papers immediately but that the local cops were too busy to comply. That made more sense.

The police officer left. I wasn't arrested.

The police did screw up. Either that or their system for informing accused persons is in need of some serious overhauling. The summons presented to me on November 14 was dated October 16 – nearly one month previously. Somewhere along the way, the summons, which would have given me at least a little advance notice of what was coming, ended up taking a month to travel the 20 kilometres from Kelowna to Peachland.

The summons commanded me to attend the RCMP detachment in Kelowna on the morning of December 5, "...for the purposes of the Identification of Criminals Act." That made me feel awful. I hadn't even been to court but I was being treated as a criminal according to the wording.

The summons also commanded me to appear in Provincial Court in Kelowna on the afternoon of December 5. Attached to the summons was a Charges Attachment that listed the charges against me. The three charges were that between June 12 and June 27, I made, distributed and possessed child pornography.

I want to scream. I want to scream aloud from the rooftops that all I did was chat on the Internet. Sure, that person ended up being an undercover cop but it was words on a screen. There were no kids involved. There were no pictures. This is all too much. Then again, I spent so much time telling myself that I was a bad person because of the thoughts I had. Now the police were telling me that I was bad enough to warrant going to court. Maybe it's fitting.

The news hit social media almost immediately. I was not an active member on Facebook but Jackie saw a few nasty comments that were posted and those comments made us angry and sad. People had no idea what was behind the charges. They were going by sheer gut instinct and some people turned on me quickly and harshly.

One morning I checked my Twitter account and discovered someone that I had done a feel-good piece on for the local newspaper had posted to me, "You should be ashamed of yourself."

My son Garrett saw quite a few negative comments on social media about the charges. People were quick to condemn me. Garrett sent a private message to every person he saw making nasty comments and told them that the person being charged was his dad and he would appreciate the comments stopping.

Whatever happened to innocent until proven guilty in a court of law? Don't people deserve the benefit of the doubt? Don't I deserve that benefit? Shouldn't people take the long view, wait, and see what happens before jumping all over me? Apparently, some people are quick to judge. Given the charges, maybe that's reasonable. I don't know.

Within days of the news hitting local media, I shut down my social media accounts to the public. It was a protective move. I didn't need to see a bunch of negative comments. Ignorance really was bliss.

One place I couldn't shut out the comments was on a local forum I often visited to talk about the latest Okanagan news. Sure enough, a thread was started on that forum and the comments were not nice. Within days of the charges being announced I was judged, found guilty and damn near executed.

It hurt me that people jumped on the Slaughter Dave bandwagon so quickly, without much in the way of solid information on which to base their opinions. The police released scant details about the case to the media. People had no idea there were no kids involved and that the charges were based on a conversation on the Internet.

Because I now had a legal case to contend with, I decided I could not post my thoughts and views on the forum. I could not risk a defence by blabbering all over the Internet. That suited me fine, except for the fact that some people were posting willy-nilly all sorts of mean-spirited things. I had to remain silent but it wasn't easy to do so.

<> <> <>

I understood where the nasty people on social media and the local forum were coming from. It was the nature of the charges against me.

The average person was going to see, hear or read the charges against me and come to only one conclusion. Possessing child pornography means to possess pictures of naked kids or kids involved in sex acts. Distributing child pornography means to send out those same pictures over the Internet to other people. The last charge, the worst one, making child pornography, meant taking pictures of kids naked or involved in sex acts. That's what the average person would think of when they heard the charges, I was sure.

In Canada, child pornography does not necessarily mean images. It also means written words. Write words that are deemed child pornography and you are guilty of making child pornography. Send those words over the Internet and you've distributed child pornography. Have a file with those words in it and you possess child pornography. That's what I learned with a quick search on the World Wide Web. It explained everything.

I made a vow of silence when it came to the comments about me on social media and the local forum. I wanted so bad to post that the charges had absolutely nothing to do with pictures and absolutely nothing to do with any children. Hell, I wanted to scream it, but I couldn't. I knew little about court cases but I knew enough to know the first thing you do when you are in trouble is shut your damn mouth. I complied.

A month or so after the charges were handed to me there was an updated news report on the radio. The announcer said RCMP had released a further detail in the case against me and the charges involving possessing, distributing and making child pornography.

"There were no local children involved according to RCMP," the announcer said.

I'm going to scream. No! It's not that there weren't any local children involved. There were no children involved. Period. Why can't they get at least that straight?

The announcer was only parroting what the RCMP told them to say, but neither he nor the RCMP went far enough with the statement. By saying there were no local children involved it left it open for there to be non-local children involved, which was not true. It was as if the cops wanted to allay fears in the community that no local kids were involved but they stopped short of reporting the whole truth. It was maddening.

I guess because of my OCD and the constant, horrible thoughts I had in my mind, I didn't get close to many people. I was well known but that didn't mean I was close to the people around me. When I was the town's only reporter, I could walk into the local grocery store and end up having a half dozen conversations with people about the news, what town council was up to, the latest rumours and what was going on around Peachland. I used to do that a lot but that didn't mean I was close to those people.

The people I was closest to were Jackie, my two boys and my two big sisters. There was another group of people that were close: my son Garrett's friends. Many of them spent a significant amount of time at our house as they grew up. In many respects, they were surrogate sons.

By the time the charges were official, I knew what my

family truly thought about me. They were all behind me. They loved me, they cared for me, they cared about me and they stood with me while I embarked on my journey to wellness and my journey through legal troubles I was just beginning to understand.

I was concerned what the friends of my boys thought when they heard about the charges. They were all young men by the time the charges were made public. What would they think about me being charged with crimes? I felt that my predicament would erode the long friendship between them and my sons. I found out soon enough what they thought.

Five days after the news was released I received the first of a number of text messages from a friend of Garrett's. Young people text. That's what they do. In a way, it's a good thing because I treasured those texts for a long time.

"I just wanted to send you a note. Dave, you have truly been a great man in my life and someone that I looked up to in many ways. I can tell you that I won't forget that man. My heart is with you and your family. I have so much love and respect for you all. Take care of yourself and you can make it through this," read the first text.

Another friend of Garrett's texted me, "Hey dad! I want you to know how I feel about you. In the past 14 years to this very day, you have been more than just my best friends' father. You have been a father to me. You have never judged me in my faults, no matter what I did and are the only one who could joke about that with me and tell it to me straight, without ever making me feel bad. Ha ha. Words cannot describe how amazing of a man you are Dave, a father, a husband, a best friend. You have countlessly demonstrated your love for your family and for us and have been that guy who I've looked up to, to be so great with his kids and to allow them to just be who they are. And you have always shown your support for them. I've seen this first hand many times! What I'm saying Dave, dad, I love you. I love who you are and I know that you know what your identity is. And I know it's definitely not this pile of shit that's going on. I will always support you and your family through anything. You are so loved and I am so fortunate to know you and have you in my life these past 14 years. I'm so excited to see what the next 14 will be. Can't wait to see you again soon! Love your pseudo son."

Still another friend texted, "I just wanted to tell you that I don't hate you at all. I love you and I am thinking about you and feeling for yourself and the family in this hard time. Just putting it out there that I have open arms, an open heart and would be a non-judgemental ear if you ever want to talk."

It meant the world to have the full support of my family. It meant a lot to have the support of the boys who had partially grown up at our house. It gave me strength and made me feel bloody good.

I stuck close to home the week after I was charged. I went over the situation in my head and tried to figure out how I was supposed to go out in public, to be possibly recognized. *How should I react? What could I possibly say to people who did recognize me? Do I tell them the whole story or nothing?*

One thing I did do during the week after the news broke was to contact a lawyer. They say you're not supposed to look through the yellow pages to find a lawyer but that's what I did. I couldn't bring myself to call around to people I knew and ask recommendations for a good criminal lawyer.

The lawyer I called was the same lawyer I contacted back at the end of June when the police wanted to sit down for an interview. His name was Wade Jenson and he sounded calm and confident on the phone. He had said in June that under no circumstances should I consent to an interview. He added the police would be on a fishing expedition, looking for more evidence against me. His advice sounded reasonable as all hell back then, so I decided to contact him again.

I was deeply concerned what the media would do, if and when, I ended up stepping into the courthouse. I could end up being the star attraction in a three-ring media circus, with reporters jostling for a comment and cameras pointed in my face.

Wade allayed my fears at least in the interim. There was no need for me to appear in court on December 5 as the summons commanded. Instead, Wade would represent me at a very preliminary hearing. I could stay home. I relaxed with that news.

Wade Jenson became my lawyer.

One thing Wade impressed upon me was that the process would be slow going. There would be delays. I would have to live with it. There was no sense in pleading guilty or trying to see if the Crown prosecutor would consider lesser charges until the case against me was disclosed.

Wade told me that the possession of child pornography charge carries a minimum sentence of three months, which can be served at the RCMP detachment in Kelowna. The other two charges, distribution of and making child pornography each carried six-month minimum sentences, which would likely be served concurrently in a provincial prison.

My heart sank.

More than anything else, Jackie and I wanted the whole situation to end. We spent five months sitting on the edge of our seats, waiting to find out what was going to happen. Now that the charges were official, we wanted it all to go away.

More than once I mentioned to Jackie that, if the cops had arrested me the day they showed up at our house with a search warrant and thrown me in jail, I would already be out and picking up the pieces of my life. The waiting was pure torture.

Wade said the Crown must disclose the evidence against me, and at some point, I would enter a plea. He said I should do nothing until the evidence was released by the prosecutor.

I was very nervous the days leading up to December 5. I may not have had to appear at the courthouse but I did have to go to the police station to be fingerprinted and have my mug shot taken. It was a mercifully short affair.

I heard nothing from Wade. By December 6, I couldn't stand it any longer. I phoned him and he seemed surprised that I wanted to know what happened. It turned out the Crown wanted more time to prepare its case and the matter was put off for four weeks.

As much as I wanted to hide at home forever and not face the world, I had to go out. We needed groceries at home and despite my life being turned upside down, life did indeed go on. I had to be a part of it. In addition, I couldn't put more responsibility on Jackie's shoulders. Her burden was enough.

All that said the first grocery shopping trip after my name was splashed all over the news was made by both Jackie and I. We went to a big grocery store in nearby West Kelowna, 10 minutes from Peachland.

I was paranoid about going out. I suspected my picture had been published along with the stories and that meant I could be easily recognized as that guy with the child porn charges.

Driving to the grocery store, I was anxious as hell. I panicked. If someone did recognize me, I didn't know what I would do. What if someone walked up to me and said something? What would I say in return? I hadn't thought it out and it scared me to think what I could face.

Inside the store, it felt like a panic attack was lurking, ready to spring forth and send me into an anxiety-induced fit. I pushed the cart while Jackie grabbed what we needed from the shelves. I kept swivelling my head around to see if anyone recognized me.

I felt like a little kid in a big, new, scary place. If someone had yelled boo, I would have jumped out of my skin. I didn't want to be in the store. I stuck close to Jackie. When we got to the checkout line Jackie decided she needed a watermelon. She started walking and disappeared down the produce aisle.

I was alone. I looked around at the people waiting in line at the various checkout counters. I glanced back at the produce aisle. I couldn't see Jackie. The panic bubbling below the surface began to boil over. I was having a physical reaction to the anxiety. I hated it. It seemed like many minutes before Jackie came back holding a watermelon. She walked up to the cart.

"Don't ever do that again," I told her. Jackie could see that I was upset. She said she was sorry and promised to stick close to me if I felt panicky again.

I spent my time at home, staying away from news reports and trying my damndest to relax. My anxiety level remained high. I did my deep breathing exercises. I remembered what I learned in relaxation therapy and put it into practice.

Soon enough it was my turn to go to the grocery store on my own. I was panicky driving to the store. I still had no idea what I would do or say if someone recognized me and said something to me about the charges against me.

Exactly nothing happened. No one in the store showed any interest in me whatsoever. No one acknowledged me, save the cashier when she looked at me and said, "Hi."

I went around the store with a list. I put items in my cart. I walked around and got what we needed. I went to the checkout, paid for my order, boxed up my goods and went back out to the car. Nothing untoward happened. Several more times I went out, sometimes to the grocery store, sometimes to other stores, and I got exactly the same response each time.

One night sitting in the Oasis, I told Jackie that I had worried about it all for nothing. Sure, my face and story were splashed all over newspapers and the nightly news for a day, but that was a week ago and other stories had taken top billing. I was no longer the story of the day. Sure, people knew about the charges against me but, the average person on the street was carrying on with their lives without any concern for me.

It was a great time to do what I had pretty much been doing since the day the police showed up at my door. I kept going.

One of my favourite quotes of all time comes from the wildly popular author of the Harry Potter series of books, J.K. Rowling: "And so rock bottom became the solid foundation on which I rebuilt my life."

I found myself at rock bottom when I was lying under the burned out log next to the creek in June. I was near rock bottom the day I found out the charges against me and my name was all over the news. Rock bottom. Can't get any worse. The bottom of the barrel.

I used to say, "The great thing about being at the bottom of the barrel is the only way out is up." The only thing is I didn't know how deep the barrel could be.

I had no idea what my life would be like in the future. I had no idea what life had in store for me, what I'd be doing for a job, how I would make an income. However, I began to see that, one way or the other, life would keep moving on. Life would continue and so would mine, if I let it.

So what I did was put one foot in front of the other. It didn't matter where I went, so long as I kept moving.

Chapter 16
Communications

My life in the spring of 2014 was spent learning about OCD, reading about other people's experiences with the disorder on forums and putting one foot in front of the other. It didn't involve working.

As much as we really needed the money and even though I was relaxed and focused, I could not see myself working out there in the world until my legal problems were resolved. One quick Google search by a prospective employer would lead to the charges against me. I couldn't see anyone hiring me. Questions would be asked. Answers would be hard to come by.

I started going to more stores and there were times when I got a dirty or odd look from someone but there was absolutely nothing I could do about how people reacted to me. I had to keep on keeping on.

The thread on the local forum was alive and well. I checked it from time to time, perhaps because I was a sucker for punishment. The comments were cruel, not based entirely on fact, and hurtful. Since looking at that particular forum always brought me down, I stopped looking at it. I decided what I couldn't see couldn't hurt me.

Spring comes early in the Okanagan Valley. It's not uncommon to see people wearing shorts in February, though it can snow in March. By the time April comes, spring is usually well set. The days get longer and the weather becomes balmy. It's a month to be outdoors and to work outdoors.

We cleaned up the Oasis in April. Vestiges of the previous fall's leaf production were in evidence all over the yard. There was lots of cleaning to be done outside and weeding needed in the back garden. We were regularly sitting outside and enjoying the mostly sunny days. We had an itch to set out bedding plants in our planters and in the back garden but that would have to wait. There were still nighttime temperatures approaching the freezing mark.

One thing Jackie and I talked about a lot was how not only did we give the police very little information the day they arrived at our house (and in my case no information because I had gone missing) but the police didn't have any information about my mental disorder.

Of course, the police couldn't have been informed about my OCD because, technically, I didn't find out about it until a month after they were at our house.

Chances are if the cops had known about my having a mental disorder and I was able to explain what I had gone through for 40 years, they wouldn't have cared less. Their job was to collect evidence of crimes committed, not listen to reasons – that's the job of the courts.

My first court appearance on December 5 had been postponed by request of the prosecution. Doing so contributed to the anxiety Jackie and I felt. The last thing we wanted was for the case to drag on.

In total, the prosecution delayed my case four times. Four times the matter was before the court in Kelowna and four times the prosecution asked for a postponement. Four times Jackie and I had to steel ourselves, only to be told by my lawyer Wade that absolutely nothing happened, and to go back to our lives.

Finally, in April we got a call from Wade. He had received a package from the Crown prosecutor detailing the evidence against me. I raced to his office.

The evidence against me as presented by the prosecution was scant and not surprising. Notes from the police in the package described how a chat conversation allegedly took place in June of the previous year between an undercover police officer and someone else. That someone else had an IP address. A search with an internet provider led to my address.

The package confirmed what I already knew. There were no children involved in the case against me. There were no images involved in my case. It all boiled down to one conversation held on the Internet. Making child pornography, according to the evidence, meant writing words. Distributing child pornography meant sending the words over the Internet. Possessing child pornography meant having a log file of the conversation.

Attached to the evidence package was a copy of the log file of the conversation from the chat room. I couldn't look at it. Things had drastically changed since I was chatting on the Internet. I was diagnosed with OCD. I had been put on two medications that were tweaked until I lost more than 80 per cent of my obsessions. I participated in relaxation therapy and Exposure and Response Prevention Therapy. I had dozens of appointments with my therapist and my psychiatrist. Any compulsive pull I used to have to chat on the Internet was long gone. My head was no longer filled with vile images and thoughts involving kids. I was in a different place and in a different time. I really didn't want to see what was. My focus was on the future.

One interesting bit of news that came out of the evidence package was the Conditions for Bail that was attached. Reading through the police notes it was clear the police went to a justice of the peace and requested an arrest warrant for me. If it was found an arrest warrant wasn't appropriate, the police asked for a summons instead. I got a summons back in November.

The police asked, according to the evidence package, for several stipulations, including that I not be in the presence of anyone under the age of 16 unless accompanied by their parent, that I visit a probation officer regularly and that I not have access to the Internet, either on a computer or on any mobile device.

When I saw the bail conditions in the evidence package, I asked Wade if that meant I was under conditions. I added that I had never seen the conditions anywhere until I saw them in the evidence package.

"You mean you were never given the conditions?" asked Wade.

I told him no. The police didn't give me anything. I asked him if they were brought up at any of the multiple hearings that had been postponed by the prosecution. He said no.

"Well we're not going to tell the prosecution they screwed up," said Wade, who indicated it is normal in cases such as mine for the accused to be put under such conditions.

I felt lucky that I wasn't under conditions but the whole thing presented a problem. Jackie and I became immediately paranoid about the bail conditions. It struck us that someone out in the public who knew about the charges against me might also know that it is normal for people like me to be put under conditions. That could mean if I did something that seemed like I shouldn't be doing, that person could contact the police and complain. The police might look into the situation, discover the conditions had never been set in place, then contact the prosecutor and suddenly I would be put under conditions.

Paranoia reigned for quite some time at our house. I wasn't around any kids so that wasn't a problem. There was nothing I could do about seeing a probation officer. The biggest problem was having access to the Internet.

The only thing I did on the Internet from the Day from Hell onward was to do some searching and reading of web pages about OCD, a daily trip to Google News to read the news headlines and reading and answering posts on the OCD-UK forum. At the time, I was only doing so on my cell phone, so I made a point of being careful using my phone in public, lest someone see me and complain to the cops.

In the 10 months since the Day from Hell, I had not

chatted on the Internet. The urge to do so was strong in the months immediately after the cops showed up at my door, but the urge waned over time and became nonexistent by the time my psychiatrist and I had my medications sorted out.

The chat conversation on the Internet was at the center of the charges against me. No doubt, the content of that conversation was disgusting and vile. I couldn't remember what that particular conversation was about but given the dark place I was at on the Internet, it would have involved children and sex. As disgusting a topic it must have been, it was no more disgusting and vile than what had been going through my head since I was in high school.

I had repugnant, loathsome thoughts about kids (and many other subjects) for nearly 40 years. Only because of the police coming did I go to Kelowna Mental Health in crisis. That led to a diagnoses of OCD and the understanding that all those disgusting thoughts I had over the years were due to a disorder I didn't know I had. The chat conversation was, in fact, a written down version of the same kind of thoughts I'd had for four decades. What Jackie and I talked about before and a lot after the evidence package arrived is that I was being charged for having OCD thoughts.

It was a different way of looking at the situation. In the beginning, when Jackie and I first started talking about it, I don't think we were all that convinced that what we were saying was true. As time went on, we started to see that, in my case, in this one case, the Canadian legal system was coming after me because I chose to write the thoughts caused by a mental disorder.

This realization turned out to be freeing. I had a mental disorder and that disorder made me think things I would have given anything to get rid of. I was completely sure that, if it weren't for the bad thoughts I used to have, I would not have been on the Internet chatting about the taboo subject.

There was a slight change in our thinking from that point on. No longer was all this about me versus the judicial system. Now mental health was involved.

"You have to stand up for mental illness," Jackie said, more than once to me.

It took a while for Jackie's words to sink in. Really, she was right. I would not be in trouble if it weren't for OCD, a mental disorder. By standing up for myself, I would also be standing up for mental illness.

Jackie and I met Wade in his small office in Kelowna in late April. Now that the evidence against me was revealed, Wade needed me to enter a plea, which was on the agenda for the next court appearance. He advised pleading not guilty. He said a plea could be changed at any time. I nodded my head and told Wade to plead not guilty.

The situation with the police, the Internet chat, the child sexual abuse thoughts and the OCD was strange to say the least.

I was trying to wrap my head around the whole situation when Jackie raised the issue that my lawyer didn't really have a good grasp of the situation. I had broached the subject of being diagnosed with him, the subsequent treatment, the improved mood and reduction in thoughts, but I hadn't really explained the situation to him in detail.

With Jackie's urging, I set out to inform Wade the best

way I knew how. I'm a writer. I sat down at our computer and started writing a document for my lawyer that would lay everything out in the open.

'Morbid Obsessions: An OCD Brief' ended up being 13 pages long and included everything I knew up to that point in time. I don't know if clients ever give detailed briefs to their lawyers but it seemed like the right thing to do in my case.

"The purpose of this brief is to bring to light certain realities the police were not aware of either prior to or subsequent to the execution of the search warrant. I was also not aware of these realities either. It was only after seeking professional help that I became aware of mental health issues that are the basis of this brief. Since this information was not available to police, it could not have been forwarded to the Crown for consideration in the laying of charges," stated the brief's introduction.

I explained in the brief how I came to be in my psychiatrist's office and how I was diagnosed with OCD. The brief then detailed the treatment I received, including medications, relaxation therapy and Exposure and Response Prevention Therapy.

A primer on what Obsessive Compulsive Disorder is followed, as did a description of how the disorder had affected my life prior to treatment. Following was a list of seven of my most troubling obsessions including morbid obsessions – those thoughts that involved harm to others and pedophilia.

On the subject of how OCD affected me I wrote, "I was a prisoner to my own thoughts. For nearly as long as I can remember, I thought poorly of myself. I thought I was one sick, depraved individual to be walking around thinking what I was thinking. Like most everyone with OCD, deep down I recognized there was something wrong with my thoughts. On the other hand, after having my psyche assaulted by intrusive, horrific thoughts day after day, I started to believe I was the person my thoughts depicted.

"Without the knowledge of my disorder I thought, if I think about hurting and killing people, I must be a murderer. If I frequently think about molesting children, I must be a child molester. After the thirtieth time seeing myself stand up in a classroom and swearing my head off, I must be that guy, right?

"I've gone through life thinking I'm a bad guy. While people around me have expressed their love and appreciation for who I am, inside my head I was thinking, Boy if they only knew."

I even discussed Maladaptive Daydreaming in the brief to Wade and briefly discussed chatting on the Internet and how my psychiatrist had said it was all OCD.

I dropped the brief off at Wade's office, hoping he would take the time to read it. A week later, I had a phone conversation with him. He called the brief very interesting. Not long after he said we should keep the not guilty plea in place and, at trial, push for a not guilty verdict because of a mental disorder.

With a not guilty plea entered, the court set a date of October 8 and 9 for a two-day trial in Provincial Court.

Until closer to the trial there was little to do but wait and try to carry on with life the best we could.

Following the success of the brief I wrote for Wade, Jackie and I decided it was time to let some of our friends know about my situation.

No one knew our side of the story. The media reported one side of the story, people were left to wonder and there was no explanation from me. I suspect that's the way it ends up being for many criminal cases but Jackie and I felt there were at least some people who deserved to know the truth.

Chief among those who deserved to hear more than what the media reported was Jackie's friends. The same friends who were coming to our house before my case hit the news were still coming to our house after. They deserved to hear something.

I sat at the computer and wrote a letter that either Jackie or I read to the friends...

April 28, 2014

By now, you've learned some disturbing things about me by word of mouth, on the news or in the newspaper. You're probably wondering what the hell is going on. You might be wondering how I am doing and, especially, how Jackie and our sons are coping with this devastating change to our lives.

Because I have a matter before the courts, I cannot discuss much about my case. I can however enlighten you about a few things. It would make Jackie and I feel better if you knew more, especially the parts left out of recent media reports.

On June 27, 2013, the RCMP came to our door armed with a search warrant. They took a computer with them. Five months later, I was formally charged with possession of, distribution of and making child pornography. That's about all that has been reported in the media.

Those charges, especially making child pornography,

likely bring to mind some awful images. The thought of making child pornography raises the issue of taking pictures of children. In Canada, child pornography also covers written material and that is what is behind my case. There were no children photographed. There were no children involved, at all, at any time.

The prosecution has disclosed the evidence against me. It centers around alleged conversations made on the Internet. 'Making' refers to writing words. 'Distribution' refers to sending those words over the Internet. 'Possession' refers to a file containing those words.

I have never and will never harm a child. Because of the laws in Canada protecting the identity of harmed children, had there been any children involved in my case, my name likely would not have been released to the media the way it was. I am facing some serious charges that carry stiff penalties if I am convicted. On the other hand, this entire ordeal has brought with it a silver lining.

Since the age of 11, I kept a secret from my family members and friends. I told no one that I had raging thoughts invading my mind that raised my anxiety level extremely high and caused me to ruminate (think deeply) for hours and hours on end.

After the police came to my door, I sought mental health help because I was in crisis. I was subsequently diagnosed by a psychiatrist as having an extreme case of Obsessive Compulsive Disorder. That's right, I have a mental disorder and I kept it secret for 40 years.

There's a lot of misinformation out there about OCD. I don't wash my hands 30 times a day, though many people do. I have no problem shaking hands or using public washrooms. What I did have is intrusive, often harmful thoughts enter my mind nearly all the time. They caused me a great deal of distress that I worked hard to hide.

I say I did have these thoughts because over the summer and fall of 2013 things changed. I participated in relaxation therapy to help calm me down. I was put on medication to fight the OCD. I also participated in a nine-week Exposure and Response Prevention Therapy course that was specifically designed for people suffering from OCD.

I am happy to say that, between the four pills I take every day and therapy, the vast majority of those awful thoughts are gone. I can focus and concentrate now, as I haven't done since I was a young kid.

Outside the stress I feel over my court case, I am doing great. I actually feel better today than I have in 40 years. And my relationship with Jackie and my two sons is stronger today than it ever was.

My family is 100% supportive of me. They fully understand what is going on, what I have gone through, how my mental health disorder has influenced my choices and the work I have done to get better.

Jackie and I have never been closer. She has been a real trooper, staying strong when I needed her most. We share, we laugh, we cry, together.

I know some people, maybe even a lot of people, think I'm some sort of evil bad guy who hurts kids. I'm not. I'm still the same guy I was a year ago, going through a tough time while trying to fully come to grips with a crushing mental disorder.

As a reporter I loved telling the whole story, from all sides. I wanted to make sure you had both sides of this story so you can make up your own mind as to what the truth is.

Chapter 17
Delays

Our home faced Beach Avenue. On the other side of the road was Okanagan Lake. We were situated all of 10 metres from the beach. When we opened up the picture window curtains, we could see a spectacular view that took our breath away.

It used to be that most evenings in the summer we would sit on our front patio and look out at the lake and mountains that surround it. It decompressed us from hectic days and grounded us to the beautiful valley in which we lived. Over the years, Peachland went from a tranquil, peaceful place in the summer to a busy, tourist laden Mecca. There were a whole lot of people on Beach Avenue in the summer and if the temperature was hot enough, the beach was as packed as a sardine can.

That's one reason why we built the Oasis in our back

yard. We wanted a place where we could relax, a refuge from the hectic life in the Okanagan in the summer.

In early May, we went to the nursery and bought our bedding plants. Jackie did her yearly planting. In our black, plastic urns, she planted Dracaena spikes in the center surrounded by portulaca and petunias. The back garden got a plethora of miniature snapdragons and we set out hanging baskets of mini-petunias and more snapdragons. In a matter of a few hours our drab spring back yard was transformed into our flower festooned Oasis.

The summer of 2014 was beautiful in Peachland. The sun shone bright and strong. Birds filled the air and seemed to spend a lot of time in and near our back yard.

There was absolutely nothing to do when it came to my legal case. The date was set for my trial and I knew I wouldn't be getting together with my lawyer Wade until closer to the trial date. I suspected we would be sitting down together to discuss strategy and the case in general but that was months away.

In the meantime, Jackie and I continued with life. We had no choice otherwise. The farther we got from that awful day in November when the charges against me hit the news, the better. We relaxed and relaxed some more. October was too far away to worry about. We found ourselves in a good, calm time and place. We spent a lot of time in the Oasis. What had been built to shelter us from the insanity of Peachland in the summer became our refuge from legal troubles.

The Oasis became the focal point as we awaited the trial. I may not have been working but I was doing something on a daily basis that was far more important. I was recovering. I was recovering from a devastating mental disorder that had trapped me in my own mind for the better part of four decades.

Jackie and I continued to talk regularly. We talked about me writing a book about my experience with OCD and how getting lost in the disorder led to my legal problems. We talked of a life altered by OCD and how much better I was doing without obsessions and compulsions taking up all my time. We even tread on what had been shaky ground for a year – the future.

No one knows what the future holds. I certainly didn't know if I was headed to jail or what my life would be like after all my legal problems were resolved. At the same time, I found myself feeling more positive than I ever had in my life. It could have been expected that I would feel depressed and anxious but instead I found myself feeling free – free from the ravages of the disorder, free from crushing anxiety and free to choose a path for my life.

Yeah but the future is unknown. I can look forward to hopefully living a life free from OCD and that is a good thing but what else is out there? I've been charged with crimes. I have a trial coming up. What will the outcome be? What will happen to me? What if I'm found guilty? What then will the future hold? I can't see a future past my trial in October.

Jackie said more times than I can count that she could see me standing on a stage somewhere telling my story and helping sufferers and others to understand OCD. Truth be told, I could see myself doing the exact same thing.

I became a regular contributor on the OCD-UK forum and felt humbled when I read the stories of other sufferers. Some days I felt a little sad that so many people were in pain. Most days I felt confident answering questions and hopeful that my words were having a positive impact on someone.

In the summer of 2014, I realized that, whatever the future held, it would continue to include OCD for me. Perhaps I'd no longer be a sufferer. But I could become an ex-sufferer impacting the lives of other sufferers. The more I thought about it, the more I realized that a book about my experience was the right thing to get working on. It would likely only end up as one step on my journey to tame the disorder and share the news with others.

I stopped by Wade's office before the September long weekend to make a payment on my account.

Not working for a year, Jackie and I didn't have two nickels to rub together. Luckily my sister Janet and brother-in-law Floyd decided my fight for mental health was worthy of their investment. They kicked in the money for my lawyer. If not for them, I don't know what we would have done.

I was asked to sign a medical records waiver so he could get access to my psychiatrist's notes about my visits to him and to get my psychiatrist to write a letter about me.

Wade had told me previously that he intended to call my psychiatrist to the stand to testify on my behalf. The reasons were clear. It was my psychiatrist who diagnosed me as having OCD and who repeatedly told me that everything, even the chatting on the Internet, was because of OCD.

When an expert witness is going to be called to the stand, the other side in the trial must be given advance warning. I guess that's so the other side can have its own expert ready to go if needed to provide contrarian evidence.

I signed the paper and then Wade let me in on something that initially floored me. He said his intent was to get my psychiatrist to write a letter about my situation prior to the trial. He would give the letter to the prosecution in my case. There was a small chance that the prosecutor in the case would look at the letter from my psychiatrist and my situation and decide to drop the charges against me.

Oh my god! Drop the charges against me? My heart's pounding. I never thought of that. Here Wade just told me this could all be over soon. No trial. No criminal record. Wow wouldn't that be something. But wait. He said it was a small chance. What the hell. A small chance is better than no chance. Drop the charges. Oh man. I hope.

From that point, every time I was in the Oasis relaxing I would close my eyes and try to send a message out to the universe: *I've suffered enough. It's all OCD. Drop the charges.*

That's what I thought, over and over again.

We hadn't heard anything from Wade for two weeks so I called him. There was less than a month to go before the trial, I reminded him. What's going on? He told me nothing was going on, that he hadn't received a letter from my psychiatrist yet. He said there was no sense in sitting down to discuss the case until that letter arrived and he had a chance to present it to the prosecution.

I asked Wade what happens if the letter doesn't arrive until close to the trial. He said it wasn't a problem. If it got to close to the trial date, he'd go down to the courthouse and book another trial date.

Another trial date?

While I understood Wade's motive behind getting the letter first, the thought of waiting longer did not appeal to me. I waited five months from the time the cops came to my door to the time charges were laid. I then waited nearly another five months to get a trial date. Then there was a third five-month period between the trial date being set and the actual trial. Fifteen months of waiting in total. It seemed a long time to me.

The inevitable happened September 26. I got a call from Wade. What he said did not surprise me.

"I didn't get the letter from your psychiatrist so I went down to the courthouse today and adjourned the trial," said Wade.

With 12 days to go before my trial was set to start, everything was put on hold, yet again.

I understood the situation from Wade's point of view, which was inevitably my point of view. No information had yet surfaced from the psychiatrist who diagnosed with me. It was going to be a critical part of my defence. We needed the information from my psychiatrist – information only he could provide. Critical would be his statement that all of it was OCD. Without that information, there is no way we could put together a defence. The trial had to wait.

Wade told me that it was no problem with postponing the trial. I asked him with not just a bit of concern in my voice how long it would be before the trial would be scheduled to proceed. I thought he would say weeks to maybe a month or so.

"Oh it will be spring for sure," said Wade.

Spring? It was the end of September. I'd have to wait months? My heart sank when I heard the news. I wasn't looking forward to going on trial for something that was wrapped up in a mental disorder, but the thought of waiting for who knew how long was a bit depressing. There was nothing I could do.

On a wall in our kitchen sits a whiteboard that we put up to write notes to each other and jot down the odd inspirational saying. Given what we had gone through since the Day from Hell, we needed inspirational sayings now and again. At the top of the white board was written the Serenity Prayer, which I learned as a child.

God,

Grant me the serenity to accept the things I cannot change,

Courage to change the things I can,

And wisdom to know the difference.

After Wade's phone call, I needed some serenity. There was not a thing I could do to speed up my trial. I was at the mercy of other people. My psychiatrist had yet to respond to the query from my lawyer and that meant we simply could not go to trial.

It had already been 15 months since the Day from Hell. If Wade was right and it would be spring before my trial, I could conceivably wait 20 months for a resolution to my legal problem. It was a lot to absorb.

Wade said something else after dropping the bomb about the new trial date. He said he would likely not be in any rush to schedule a new date because he would want to make darn sure he had his ducks in a row with my psychiatrist. In addition, he said during the intervening time between my first and second trial dates, it might be good for me to go see another psychiatrist. Two opinions for a defence would be better than one.

Oh, crap. That's what I thought when I picked up the local newspaper in Peachland one week after the phone call from Wade. My name was in the news again. A small article appeared on Page 2. The article stated I was due in court the following Wednesday to set a time for a trial date. The reporter missed the fact that that Wednesday had been the day for a trial and since I was now due to appear to have a trial date set that meant my trial had been postponed. They completely missed that little fact.

Wade had said that my trial date would likely be used to schedule a new trial date, so that matched what the article stated. The fact the article appeared at all saddened both Jackie and I.

We wanted this legal situation over but we were wallowing in a quagmire that we couldn't get out of because other people were pulling the strings. In the meantime, any media outlet could jot down an article at anytime, stirring the pot a little more and reminding us that I could be the subject de jour, to be resurrected at anytime like a meaty sparerib from a barbeque, there to titillate the hunger of those eager to know what's going on.

It pissed me off to see the article. It pissed me off more to know that the vast majority of people in my town knew nothing of my story, nothing of what I went through in the past 15 months. At that point in time, I wanted to change the situation. I was convinced the right thing to do was to pound the pavement and talk to anyone who would listen.

I called Wade. I asked him directly, "What am I allowed to say to people?"

Going further, I told Wade that people probably had an impression that, given the charges against me, I had some dark dungeon under my house where I photographed nude kids doing sex acts. He was very understanding of my concern and diplomatic in his answer. The short of it was he told me to shut up.

Wade said he understood that I might want to tell a select few people my side of the story but, "You never know who's listening in."

That was great. Save for a very few people to whom we had explained my situation, I had been silent for 15 months. Now my lawyer was telling me to stay silent for many more months.

To a certain extent, I understood what Wade meant about not letting the cat out of the bag when it came to my future defence. We didn't want the prosecution to know what my defence would be until it was time. Although I didn't discuss the matter with Wade, I supposed we did not want the prosecution to have months and months to prepare a killer cross-examination of my witnesses that would crush my defence based on having a mental disorder. On the other hand, at the very least, I wanted people to know what the charges really meant, what they were based on (a conversation on the Internet) and most importantly, what they were not about.

Before the conversation ended, Wade told me that he did have a conversation with my psychiatrist. My psychiatrist told Wade that, although he was a psychiatrist, he was not a forensic psychiatrist – a doctor of the mind who is also familiar with legal matters.

I didn't really understand the distinction but Wade said it wasn't a problem – he had several forensic psychiatrists he could call upon. It seemed apparent I would be explaining my former situation with yet another psychiatrist. The idea of explaining my life to a second psychiatrist so he could understand where I came from so he could determine whether I was mentally something or another did not appeal to me.

I'm feeling so doubtful. What if this second psychiatrist hears my story and comes up with a different conclusion than my psychiatrist? What if he decides that OCD didn't have that much of an effect on me? What if he decides chatting on the Internet and having sexual thoughts about children has nothing to do with OCD? What then?

It was one more thing to worry about. Apparently, I had time on my side. All I could do was wait.

Fall in the Okanagan Valley is a beautiful thing. While temperatures at night slowly dipped lower, leaves refused to lose their grasp on branches. Trees stayed green well into November.

By early November all that remained that made the Oasis an oasis was one hanging basket of petunias. Our Hosta had turned brown, wilted and died back. Snapdragons that had populated the back garden were pulled and sent to the compost site. A sole hanging basket of brilliant purple flowers hung on its hook off the back fence.

Finally, in mid-November, the temperature plunged over successive nights below freezing. The purple flowers of the hanging basket shrivelled and died, while the foliage took on a brownish-grey hue. It was the end of the back yard as Oasis and the beginning of winter proper.

During the second week of November, I received a letter from Wade. My new trial date was set for August 31, 2015.

I wasn't sure if I should laugh or cry. My trial was now set nine months in the future. There would be nine more months of waiting, nine more months of having a tough time finding a job, nine more months of relying on Jackie's income solely to get us through each month, nine more months of not knowing what the future held.

In total, it would be 26 months from the Day from Hell to my trial.

I became disillusioned for a few days. All I wanted was for this part of my life to be over, one way or the other. I was at the mercy of the Canadian legal system and my fate was at the whim of lawyers.

Many times in my life a situation could emerge that would send me into a tailspin of high anxiety, depressed mood and raging thoughts. They were the times when I felt the lowest. Even when the situation in hindsight was not particularly earth shattering in nature, I could wind up despondent. I'm sure having to deal with OCD had much to do with that.

Things change.

I was so despondent when the police showed up at my house in June 2013 that I contemplated suicide. Shortly thereafter, I was diagnosed with OCD and began taking medications and receiving treatment. I experienced let downs after but it seemed like each time I did I was able to recover more quickly.

Having to face my demons in the burned-out log beside the creek was devastating. Finding out I was being charged with a crime as the whole world found out too was nearly as devastating. Each successive let down, like finding out the evidence against me, having to wait five months until my trial and having my trial postponed were a little less troubling, a little easier to handle.

Then I found out my trial would be postponed another

nine months. It hurt, but it didn't hurt all that much. Within days of receiving the news from Wade, I was pretty much back to the same levelheaded, calm person I had become.

Chapter 18
The Plan

Two things marked the summer of 2015: the heat and the steady march toward my trial date.

Spring was a marginal enterprise with warmish temperatures during the day and cool nights. I commented to Jackie sometime in June that it seemed like spring was taking forever to finish. We settled in new plants in our Oasis garden and planters and worked like mad to make our grass look like a lawn.

About the third week in June, everything changed. It was as if someone flipped a switch and the sun turned on for real. Suddenly temperatures were pushing 30 C or beyond and for months we basked and baked in the Okanagan sun. At times, it got so hot it was all we could do to stroll across the street and jump in the lake to cool off. It got to 39 C during the summer. Although I was indoctrinated in the ways of Celsius and the metric system in junior high school, I still from time to time converted to Fahrenheit for the fun of it and realized the thermometer had surpassed 102 degrees on the old scale. Smoking hot.

The last I heard from my lawyer Wade was that he was thinking it would be a good idea for me to sit down with another psychiatrist who would then testify on my behalf. That was back in November the previous year. As the long, hot summer days of 2015 pressed on, I wondered what happened to that idea.

My two-day trial was scheduled to begin August 31. By the middle of July, I had heard little from Wade. I was having serious reservations about my choice in legal representation. What was going on? What was my defense going to be? Who would be called to the witness stand? Would I have to testify? What was happening with the mysterious psychiatrist my lawyer had lined up to testify? Did I have a hope in hell?

I did not want to sit on my hands before the trial and then have a flurry of activity just days before the trial. Wade had assured me that would not be the case. He said we would have plenty of time to sit down and talk about the case and everything would go splendidly.

I started to get concerned.

No longer content to wait, I picked up the phone and called Wade. He assured me that things were progressing as they should and there was still plenty of time before the trial to sit down together. I mentioned that I had written the first draft of a book, although there were chapters yet to be written because it all depended on the outcome of my legal case. Wade was intrigued. He asked if he could get a copy right away.

I was surprised Wade would be interested in a book on my experience. I was pleased to be doing something, anything, that might further my case along. I didn't know how or why my book might have relevance to my trial. I had to trust that he knew what he was doing. I printed out a copy of the book and rushed it to his office. A week or so went by and I phoned Wade. I was eager to find out what he thought of the book.

"You're obviously a talented writer," he told me. He called the book very interesting and said he thought it was something that should definitely be published.

Then we got on the subject of the mystery psychiatrist. Wade said he had been in contact with a forensic psychiatrist he had worked with before, who offered to help in my case.

For the first time, Wade explained that my defense pertained to Section 16 of the Criminal Code of Canada. Section 16 is the Canadian equivalent to the well-known American defense of not guilty by reason of mental defect. In order for a Section 16 defense to be successful, the accused must show that he both has a mental disorder and that he did not know what he was doing was wrong, Wade explained. He said he had several conversations with the forensic psychiatrist and although the psychiatrist felt he could help, Wade was unconvinced that such a defense would prove successful.

Wade indicated it could be a waste of $10,000 to $15,000 to involve the psychiatrist in my defense. I nearly choked. Jackie and I didn't have two nickels to rub together. We had already borrowed $10,000 from my sister and brother-in-law for legal representation. There was no way we were going to come up with another $10,000 to

$15,000 to hire a psychiatrist. If I didn't have a forensic psychiatrist to back up my claim of a Section 16 defense, my case would dissolve.

I had no defense.

Strangely, Wade didn't seem all that concerned. He said he had met with the Crown prosecutor several times about my case and that more meetings would be coming up, as the trial got closer.

As the day neared, the stress level in our house rose. We had been through so many legal delays that by August it was 26 months since the cops had arrived at my door and 21 months since I was formally charged with crimes. Jackie and I felt sure the August 31 trial date was final, that there would be no further delays and, one way or another, I would be in court facing the charges against me.

In the middle of August, a police officer came to the door early in the morning. He wanted to talk to Aaron. My son received a subpoena from the officer, commanding him to be in court on August 31.

Just great.

My own son was ordered to be a witness for the prosecution. Aaron was devastated. Jackie was devastated. I was devastated. Aaron told us he was worried that something he might say on the stand could go against me. We told him he would have to tell the truth, no matter what.

Exactly what the prosecution was thinking in subpoenaing my son, I didn't know. I suspected they needed someone from my house to testify whose computer the police had confiscated when they conducted a search warrant back in June of 2013.

Aaron suffers from an anxiety disorder and I was sure

the thought of testifying on the stand would send him into a panic attack. I didn't know what to do. My stress level reached new heights. I called Wade to tell him about the subpoena.

And everything changed. Wade told me not to worry, that everything was going to plan.

Plan? What Plan?

Then Wade explained what he had been working on. I was floored.

Chapter 19
Assessment

One piece of advice I gave often on the OCD-UK forum was for sufferers to try to find a qualified OCD therapist so they can get the right treatment for their disorder, namely Cognitive Behavioral Therapy. It's the right advice to give because so many people need help to deal with their OCD. Usually, that means going to see a general practitioner as a first step. The idea is that the GP will assess the situation and send the sufferer to someone qualified to deal with OCD. It doesn't always work out that way.

Brian posted at the end of July about his experience in seeking help for his OCD. He exhibited the classic signs of having pedophile obsessions, just as I did. His thoughts were such that he thought he was attracted to kids, which in turn freaked him out. It's all perfectly normal in an OCD world.

"After three years of battling with my own thoughts, and being scared to death of being attracted to kids, I decided to see my GP and get some help," wrote Brian.

"A couple of weeks ago I went to an assessment appointment with a young woman and I told her about my worries and my thoughts. I laid everything down on the table," said Brian. "I left with the impression she didn't really understand what I was talking about."

A few days after his initial assessment, Brian got a phone call from a man at a mental health access team asking him to go to another appointment. "There are a few things that you have disclosed that concern us," the man told Brian. The search for help for his OCD quickly spun out of control for Brian. He was told at his second meeting that thoughts of children were very concerning to the team and they wanted to assess him further. A safeguarding agency had been contacted to start a program with Brian. Reading between the lines, the access team had contacted the authorities about Brian being a danger to children.

"I told him I had a real fear of being attracted to underage girls," wrote Brian. "I told him that I can't stand to be in the same room as a child. I don't think he understood. He asked me whether I thought I had split personality. He even gave me the number and website address of an organization that specializes in helping pedophiles. Absolutely unbelievable."

Brian felt that he was being monitored by the authorities. He worried that his Internet usage was being monitored and his communications. "As you can imagine, I'm in a real spin," he said. "I can't bring myself to eat and I'm not breathing properly. I always feared something like this happening and it seems it has."

One of my greatest fears over the years was that people would find out about my thoughts and I would be locked up in jail or in a mental institution for having thoughts about kids and sex. That's one of the reasons I kept my thoughts a secret for nearly 40 years. It's a common fear among OCD sufferers, especially those who suffer from pedophile obsessions.

Fear turned into reality for Brian. It was unclear what level of proficiency the people Brian met with had but it was very clear they had no experience dealing with sufferers of OCD.

I wrote to Brian, "From time to time this type of situation happens. It sucks. Some people just don't understand the disorder and don't understand the pedophile theme and they misconstrue what they hear and all of a sudden, they're pushing the panic button. You don't need the help of these people. They are clearly not the type of people you need to be dealing with."

I felt very sorry for Brian. He started looking for help and he ended up scared that he was being branded a pedophile. What's more, Brian's situation led me to believe other people could hear about his story and decide they wouldn't seek help for fear of being treated as badly as Brian was. Shortly after posting about his problem, Brian stop posting. I wondered often what happened to him.

Brian's story stuck with me. There was a parallel to my own story. Since I was about 15, I was struck by intrusive thoughts about children and sex. They were, along with the hurt-thoughts, the scariest thoughts I had. They were so scary that I couldn't bring myself to tell anyone about them. For decades, I believed if I told about my thoughts, I would be arrested, thrown in jail or committed to a psychological institution. Along with fear of abandonment, this was the fear that bothered me the most. I felt like no one would understand my thoughts. I felt as if people would detest me, brand me a pedophile and lock me away. Then along came Brian with his tragic story of having his OCD misunderstood. It hit home.

My lawyer Wade had a plan. I was excited. I was floored by the possibilities the plan presented. I told Jackie the moment I heard about it and she too became excited. I phoned my two sisters, who were camping together in Alberta. Janet got excited. Barb cried. The plan was something we never would have dreamed could happen.

The plan was all Wade's. When he told me the details, I was suddenly struck by how glad I was that he was my lawyer. I realized I made some good choices along the way. Giving Wade a 16-page brief on OCD and the types of OCD I had was the right thing to do. Giving Wade the first draft of my book was the right thing to do. I gave him something to work with and something that he could base his plan on.

Both lawyers were looking at my case as something unusual. Wade had previously told me that in a search of legal cases, he could not come up with one case in Canada that matched mine, that involved chatting on the Internet about the contents of my thoughts and Obsessive Compulsive Disorder. He said my case was different and it deserved a different outcome.

Things kicked into high gear just seven days before my trial was to start. Both lawyers appeared in a Kelowna courtroom. Both lawyers agreed to adjourn my trial and requested the court order a psychiatric assessment.

<> <> <>

The prosecutor hadn't signed off on the plan. What he told Wade, even with all the information I had provided, was that he wanted something to hang his hat on. He wanted some kind of assurance that going ahead with the plan was the right thing to do, so I was headed to a psychiatric assessment. I did not know what that would entail. Clearly, I would be talking to a forensic psychiatrist. Because it was ordered by the court, taxpayers would foot the bill. I couldn't afford the bill in any event.

The big question was why exactly would I be going for an assessment and what was expected out of it? From what I had gathered from Wade and some research, it seemed that psych assessments were typically ordered to determine if someone was fit to stand trial and to determine if someone fits the bill for a Section 16 defense. In my case, the facts of the case were not in dispute. I had not actually said I was guilty and had certainly not pleaded guilty but I wasn't in disagreement with the prosecution's fundamental case. I chatted on the Internet and the words in the chat matched the definition of child pornography. In Canada, that was not legal. I suspect the prosecutor knew it. I knew I had OCD and it played a major role in events leading up to the charges against me. Wade knew it because I both told him and let him read the whole story. The prosecutor must have known because Wade said something to him and he agreed to adjourn the case in favor of a psych assessment.

As Wade said, the prosecutor wanted something to hang his hat on. What exactly was he looking for?

To the best of my knowledge, the psychiatrist who diagnosed me with OCD never did produce a letter or document that stated I had OCD. He had his notes from our many sessions in his office but no official document ever made it to the lawyers. After thinking about it for a while, I realized one thing the prosecutor would be looking for was a declaration I had OCD. That would, in essence, lend credence to the rest of my story.

My pending psych assessment would be about assessing me as I was more than two years previous. A lot had changed since the police showed up at my door. I was a calm, completely different person to the frantic, anxiety-ridden sufferer I used to be.

Ten days after the court ordered the psychiatric assessment, I received a letter in the mail. The assessment was scheduled for late September. The letter said the assessment would take one to two hours. The next day I received a phone call from a psychiatric nurse. She wanted to interview me for background information before I sat down with the forensic psychiatrist later that month.

A few days later, I met with the psychiatric nurse. She had a ton of questions for me. She wanted to know what jobs I had held, from the very first job I had packing groceries after school and on weekends, to my last job as proprietor of a news website, and every job in between. She asked about my family, every member in it, how old they were, if they were married, what they did for a living and if they had any psychological or addictions problems. The questions went on to include what disorders I had been diagnosed with, what medications I was on to how well I did in school. It took a little more than an hour. The background information phase of my assessment was done.

There were 14 days until I met the forensic psychiatrist. Everything hinged on the report that came out of that meeting.

The day before my psych assessment was not a good day. I was moody, withdrawn and nervous. I kept trying to figure out what the assessment would entail and what questions would be asked. More than two years of waiting would all boil down to whatever the assessment report stated.

What if I don't answer the questions right? What if I don't say the right things? What if I say the wrong thing? Will I screw up my chances for the future? Will I screw up my life royally? I'm scared. Everything hinges on what the forensic psychiatrist says and that all hinges on what I say. It's all up to me.

Jackie helped me to see that I was working myself up over nothing. All I had to do was answer some questions and tell my story.

The next morning I drove to Kelowna Mental Health for the first time in many, many months. I got out of the car, locked the car door and smiled when I didn't have to lock it a second time or a third. I went upstairs to the mental health unit, checked in and waited for my appointment. I was escorted to an office in the back of the building and introduced to the forensic psychiatrist. She first explained that although her office was in Kelowna Mental Health, she worked for the court system. She also explained that she was a psychiatrist with legal expertise.

Much of the first half hour was spent reviewing the information I had given to the psychiatric nurse a couple of weeks before. It became apparent early on during the interview that the forensic psychiatrist was a bit perplexed. I had no earth-shattering revelations about my childhood for her. I was not and had never been addicted to alcohol or drugs. The only thing wrong with me, at least up until two years before, was that I suffered a severe to extreme form of OCD.

She outright asked me what I thought the assessment was meant to accomplish. I told her that neither my lawyer nor the prosecutor was expecting a diagnosis of such a severe mental problem that it would render me incapable of distinguishing between right and wrong. I told her straight up I wasn't nuts but I felt the OCD severely affected my choices.

The hardest question I was asked was why I ended up chatting on the Internet. It was a tough question to answer but I did my best. I explained that, since the age of about 15, I had been inundated with intrusive thoughts involving children and sex – so much so that I had become convinced I was a pedophile. Chatting on the Internet about my thoughts seemed logical but it was also a compulsion of mine – something I figured out only after I did a lot of learning and soul-searching.

As I sat there in the small office, I wondered how long it would take me to find out what the report would say. I learned at the end of the assessment. The forensic psychiatrist told me that her report would show I did know the difference between right and wrong at the time I was chatting on the Internet. That wasn't terribly disturbing to me because the alternative was to be told I was seriously mentally ill and could wind up in an institution. She also told me that she had the notes from my psychiatrist and that her report would reflect the fact that I had a serious case of OCD but it was well managed with medication and therapy.

<> <> <>

Whipped. That's the way I felt during the evening of October 20. Barely two hours earlier, I had been surfing the Internet on my phone when I happened upon an article on a website about me.

October 20 was a court appearance date. It was a day to see if the psychiatric assessment had been completed and if the report was in. If all the ducks were in a row, I supposed the prosecutor and my lawyer would decide on where to go from there. The article was short. It explained that I had a court appearance to deal with a psychiatric assessment. Apparently the report was completed. Neither lawyer had seen the report and, of course, that meant the matter was adjourned to two weeks down the road.

I felt whipped because I was the subject of yet another media report, including a picture of me, easily taken off Facebook several years before. There I was, in black on white, my name associated with child pornography and yet another delay. The particular website that ran the story hadn't reported anything about me for about a year. For 12 blessed months, they had left me alone and gone on to other stories. Then out-of-the-blue, on a day when a minor court appearance took place (and nothing happened) they decided to resurrect my charges, my photo and my legal plight and splash it all over the front page of the website.

Every time my name appeared in any form of media, it was like picking off a scab from a deep wound. The wound opened and I bled, only the bleeding was inside.

"I'm so sick of this shit," I told Jackie.

To make matters worse, I was a hot topic again on the local forum I had come to despise. Though there were a few people on the forum who supported me and tried to balance the scales, overwhelmingly the posters who commented spoke with lynch mob qualities. I was tried, convicted and sentenced to purgatory by a jury of anonymous forum posters.

"Can they drag this on any longer? Put his ass in jail already," said one poster. While I wouldn't agree with the second statement, the first resonated with me. Dragged on was right.

Something that wasn't right was that I couldn't say a damn thing in my defence. I wanted to go on that local forum so many times and set the record straight. I wanted to type out in all caps (the equivalent of Internet shouting) that there were no kids involved, there were no pictures and all of this, as my psychiatrist had pointed out so long ago, was due to Obsessive Compulsive Disorder. There were days it took everything I had to hold back and grit my teeth. Wade made it clear. I was to say nothing. I was to suck it up and let happen whatever happened.

My name was all over the Web. Internet justice is the modern day equivalent of having ones hands and head locked in a set of stocks in the middle of the town square in the 1700s. You're on display for all to see. The difference is, centuries ago they eventually let you out of the stocks. The Internet is forever.

By October 20, I had not worked for nearly 28 months. How could I? My website imploded, leaving me without work. Five months later, I was charged and the media jumped on the story. My name was all over the Internet and not in a good way. How exactly was I going to get a job when the most cursory Google search of my name would lead to stories of charges of child pornography? Was I to submit my rather extensive resume to prospective employers and hope they didn't check me out? All it would take is one person associated with the employer to see a media story about me and it would all be over. Even after all was said and done, my legal problems were resolved, I would still face having to make a living with a very dark, very black cloud over my head.

As I had discovered many times since my tribulations began, there wasn't a damn thing I could do about my circumstance. I was afloat on a rickety boat being steered by others on an ocean of uncertainty. I could take care of myself, which I was. I could not control what others did and what others said. If the media wanted to stir the pot with another story, I could do nothing about it. Let it go. If people hiding behind anonymity wanted to bash me, I could not change it. Let it go.

To let the words and actions of others drag you down is sad. To rise above what you can't control is serenity.

Chapter 20
A Christmas Present

The psych report, which was apparently out there somewhere, was slow making its way to the Crown prosecutor and my lawyer Wade. Without the report in their hands, a decision could not be made and we could not move forward.

I busied myself in the beginning of November with winterizing our back yard, putting away our patio furniture underneath a big tarp on the side yard, packing odds and ends into our storage shed and getting rid of the rest of our annual plants that would soon freeze.

As winter approached and below freezing temperatures lurked, our Oasis became just a place with two chairs to sit. The Oasis would be dormant for four months until spring brought with it temperatures conducive to living outside.

The psych report finally arrived mid-November. I went

to Wade's office and picked up a copy. There were no startling revelations.

Overall, the report was a recap of what the forensic psychiatrist and I had discussed during our one-hour session. The psychiatrist's opinion was located at the end of the report. It comprised four short paragraphs and would be the part of the report most scrutinized by the lawyers.

"Mr. Preston gives a clear history of obsessive compulsive disorder characterized by obsessive ruminations which he dates back to approximately the age of 11," the report stated. "The types of thoughts he describes are quite classic ones, however they don't appear to have been accompanied by many compulsive rituals."

"Mr. Preston also gives a history of depressive and anxious symptoms in the past and I think would have fulfilled the criteria for panic disorder, generalized anxiety disorder and possibly major depressive disorder," the report stated. Although I was only ever diagnosed with OCD, it didn't surprise me that in the psychiatrist's opinion I suffered from more than one type of disorder.

"The medication and psychological treatment that Mr. Preston has had for his obsessive compulsive disorder appears to have treated his symptoms with good effect and he will likely need to continue on such treatment indefinitely," the report said. I agreed with that part of the report and I hope it came out from that section that I was a different person after meds than I was before.

The last part of the psychiatrist's opinion was perhaps the most crucial but there were no surprises. During my interview with her, the forensic psychiatrist explained to me that her task was to determine if I was criminally responsible for my actions while chatting on the Internet or not. She further explained that if she found I was not criminally responsible, it would mean I would probably wind up in a psych ward somewhere, as opposed to going to jail.

"I don't think his Obsessive Compulsive Disorder rendered him incapable of appreciating the nature and quality of his actions or that they were wrong," stated the report.

Although it was worded the way I suspected it would be, the psychiatrist's final opinion didn't go far enough in my mind. She was only asked if I was criminally responsible or not. She didn't delve into my assertion that chatting on the Internet was just one more compulsion derived by having a severe case of OCD. She didn't comment on whether having severe OCD could have an adverse affect on a person's judgment.

In August, I was due to go to trial over the charges against me. Wade convinced the prosecutor that my case was sufficiently different to warrant a look at a novel resolution. The prosecutor was on board, at least to the point of proceeding further and he wanted the psychiatric assessment done. The report was completed but I wasn't sure if it helped or hindered my future prospects.

One good thing that came from the report is that the prosecutor had a formal piece of paper that confirmed I had Obsessive Compulsive Disorder, which backed up my claims (communicated through Wade) that this whole mess was due to a mental disorder. The report did show that I was on medications and was doing very well on them.

I guessed it was a bad thing that the report said I was in charge of my mental faculties during the time I chatted with an undercover police officer over the Internet. On the other hand, I never thought the report would say I was nuts. I was hoping it would confirm the compulsive behavior I had come to understand.

It all boiled down to what the prosecutor in my case thought. He had the psych assessment. Who knew what he would make of it.

I hoped a decision would be soon in coming but it didn't work out that way. My case would be on the agenda from court and immediately it would be postponed. The prosecutor wasn't ready to make a decision. Time and again, my case was adjourned to a week later. I lost track how many times my case was on the court's agenda and I went online and looked it up.

By the end of November, Wade had appeared on my behalf in court 21 times.

A phone call came on December 2.

I was trying my best to find serenity, to accept the things I could not change. I could not change the slow, plodding pace of my legal case. I could not hurry up the prosecutor. I could not change the wording of the psych assessment done for me. I was trying to be peaceful while the world slowly turned but I was anxious all the same.

My anxiety level spiked when I saw on my cell phone that Wade was calling. That was it. I knew it. It was the call I had been waiting months for. I was about to find out if I was headed toward a trial or a much softer resolution that would take into account the mental disorder I had struggled so long against.

Wade told me straight up that the prosecutor had decided to accept the plan. I couldn't breathe. I couldn't comprehend that my life had suddenly changed, for the better.

There was one fly in the ointment, according to Wade. The prosecutor wanted a letter from my original psychiatrist stating the treatment I had gone under for my OCD and a statement that I was not a danger to the community.

My psychiatrist understood OCD. He's the one who looked me right in the face and told me I had suffered enough and that it was all OCD. He knew that sufferers don't do what their obsessions say. Sufferers who have obsessions about stabbing people with knives don't stab people with knives. People with intrusive thoughts about driving their cars into other cars don't drive their cars into other cars. People with pedophile obsessions don't go out and rape children. I knew that and I knew my psychiatrist knew that.

I was out when the call from Wade came and I raced home to tell Jackie. We hugged. A good, long hug. Suddenly there was light at the end of tunnel. Our by then 30-month ordeal could soon be over.

Wade had told me he would send a letter to my psychiatrist, asking for specific information to be included in a return letter. I had to go back to waiting but at least it was a type of wait with a silver lining. If the letter contained the right information, the whole mess I was in could be quietly resolved. One more step and my life could start again after two and a half years.

The anxiety I had been feeling, which seemed to get worse over time as I awaited word from the prosecutor, slowly bled away. I truly had hope on my side and with hope came peace.

<> <> <>

Our whole house was decorated for Christmas. We had our seven-foot, pre-lit, artificial Christmas tree up in the living room. It was packed with all the ornaments we had collected over a 30-year period since Jackie and I had known each other, including most of the handmade ornaments our kids had made for us in elementary school. It was cute, charming and quaint. Throughout the kitchen and living room were decorations, mostly handmade and hand painted woodcrafts that Jackie had made over the years.

Not working for two and a half years meant no money coming in by me and that meant money was tight in our house. The previous year we had so little money that we couldn't afford gifts for each other. But some amazing people we knew made Christmas happen for us by buying gifts for under our tree. For 2015, we had a few bucks available and we were able to buy some small gifts to put under the tree.

We were used to not having extravagant gifts for Christmas. For us it was more a time for family, for playing games, for having turkey dinner and for relaxing. The one thing we wanted for Christmas was an end to the legal troubles that had plagued us for 30 months.

Wade called four days before Christmas. I knew something was up. He was in a jovial mood and he told me it was a done deal. He had contacted my psychiatrist and asked him to prepare a letter answering the questions from the prosecutor. Instead of doing up a letter, my psychiatrist sent my lawyer the notes made during my sessions. Those notes were then given to the prosecutor.

The prosecutor, apparently, wasn't thrilled with the

result. What he really wanted was an up-to-date letter detailing what therapy I had gone through, what medications I was on and whether I was danger to the public going forward. Wade impressed upon him that whatever the psychiatrist's notes said, they were enough for the matter-at-hand. The prosecutor eventually agreed and said he was satisfied he had the information he needed.

I had long ago wondered what it would be like if things went my way and I imagined that I would jump up and down, scream at the top of my lungs and thank my lucky stars. Instead, I was calm. And maybe a little shocked. It was as if any residual anxiety inside me bled away like air from a slowly leaking bike tire.

Prosecutors look at a couple different things when deciding if a case should be prosecuted or not. The first is whether there is sufficient evidence that a crime has been committed. The other is whether it is in the community's interest that a crime be prosecuted. There was evidence in my case that a crime had been committed but I think the prosecutor decided, based on the evidence I have OCD and it played a major role in my chatting on the Internet, that it was not in the community's best interest to see a different outcome in my case.

There would be one final court date coming up in the New Year - one final court appearance with a twist. For that appearance, for the one and only time, I would have to appear in person.

Chapter 21
Looking to the Future

The Okanagan Valley, for all its beauty and sunshine in the summer, can be a bleak place in winter. Grey clouds consistently drift in and anchor themselves above the valley, painting a dismal, shadowed picture over the sky. Sometimes for months, the sun does not break through. But it shone on February 9.

We got our fair share of snow over the winter, perhaps a little less than normal but enough to warrant shoveling several times. By the beginning of the second week of February 2015, the snow had melted away. Spring crocuses had already pushed up from the soil and the grass in our back yard Oasis was mostly green.

It was a hint of spring after a relatively mild winter and the sun on my face felt wonderful as I pondered what was about to happen.

But for a problem with scheduling, February 9 should already have taken place. Four or five times my case came up in court and was quickly adjourned because the prosecutor did not show up at the appointed time. It turned out he was involved in a murder trial and could not get away to deal with my lesser case. It meant more waiting on my part but given that my legal ordeal had already taken more than two and a half years, a few more weeks wasn't going to cause undue hardship.

Wade first broached the subject of his innovative and distinctly different plan to the prosecutor at least as far back as July of 2014. It took seven months, a psychiatric assessment and multiple court dates to see the plan come to fruition.

I don't think I could adequately describe how indebted to Wade I was. For the longest time I had the sense that I was a spectator of my own legal case, just there for the ride, while Wade and the prosecutor haggled behind closed doors. I had no idea Wade had a plan and that he was pushing hard for that plan to be enacted. Once I found out what he was thinking, I was so, so glad I had chosen Wade Jenson to be my lawyer. He came up with something I never would have thought of in a million years. His plan would solve all the problems and, in a real way, save me.

I was due in court at 3 p.m. As the sun shone through our front window, warming our home and casting brilliant light throughout, I walked upstairs to get dressed. I don't wear dress clothes often and I had to work at fitting into my old dress pants and suit jacket. I didn't have much to choose from so I chose an all-black outfit, including black, crisp dress shirt.

Jackie came home from work early so she could be with

me. We had been together through the whole ordeal, from the cops showing up at our door to my diagnosis to the recovery from OCD and all through my legal troubles. We would be together for the final court date.

We drove into Kelowna early and it was a good thing. There was some kind of police incident going on and traffic was snarled and backed up heading into Kelowna. Still, we arrived at the courthouse with plenty of time to spare.

The courtroom was small. Wood panelling adorned the walls and the bench, which seemed much larger than what seemed appropriate for a relatively small room, was blonde wood.

Two other cases, one a theft under $5,000 and the other dealing with a father assaulting his daughter, were dealt with before my case was called. There were the judge up high behind the bench, a court reporter, Wade, the prosecutor, Jackie and I and two reporters (one recognizable from TV and the other brandishing a reporter's steno book).

Wade had told me previously that going to court on that day would simply be a matter of the judge rubber-stamping what the two lawyers already agreed to. A plan had been presented by Wade, agreed to by the prosecutor, and now the court would put it into place, officially.

The judge stated the matter before the court was an application for a Section 810.1 Recognizance. In layman's terms, the prosecutor was applying to have the three charges against me dismissed and to put in their place a peace bond. This was Wade's plan.

Peace bonds used to be issued most notably in cases of domestic abuse where, in lieu of charges and convictions, an offender could agree to a set of court ordered conditions for a period of up to a year. The conditions could take the form of abstaining from alcohol or agreeing not to have any contact or communication with the complainant. In more recent years, the role of the peace bond had been expanded to include other types of cases.

The prosecutor stood before the bench and gave the bare basics of the case against me. He told the judge about an online chat happening in June 2013 on the Internet, which led to an IP address. Police then arrived at my home with a search warrant. A file was discovered on my laptop of the chat conversation, which involved the subject of children and sex and fell under the definition of child pornography in Canada. From that came the three charges of making, distributing and possessing child pornography.

No children were involved in my case, the prosecutor pointed out. In addition, there were no pictures or videos involved. The case centered on one conversation on the Internet.

A peace bond was being sought, according to the prosecutor, because there was a mental health issue at the center of the case and because of the overwhelming amount of negative publicity my case had received, according to the prosecutor.

Wade spoke for a few minutes. He told the court that OCD was involved in my case and he added that the whole thing was a mixed blessing because, although the police were involved, it ended up that I sought mental health help and was subsequently diagnosed with OCD and that allowed me to get better from a mental health standpoint.

I sat in front of the bench, beside Wade, through all of it. There wasn't much for me to say. I glanced over and saw the reporters madly scribbling in their books. Jackie sat behind me watching.

Much of the 25 minutes we spent in court was devoted to what conditions would become part of the peace bond and how they should be worded. One thing that came up that made me shake my head was the prosecutor's reference to my being arrested. Several media outlets had reported that too and the fact was I was never arrested. I didn't bother to correct the prosecutor.

At the end of the session, I was asked if I agreed to the conditions as set out and I said, "Yes, your honour."

It was over. I turned around. Jackie was standing. She held her hand high, I grabbed it, and then kissed her. My legal ordeal, our legal ordeal, was over. We were, for the briefest time, exuberant because two and a half years of stress and worry was at an end. And we were happy because mental health, in a small way, won.

The three charges against me were dropped. They no longer existed. I had to comply with the conditions of the peace bond but I would have no criminal record. I would not have my name added to any sex offender database. I would not have to give a DNA sample to the police. In fact, once the peace bond expired in one year, I would be able to petition the police to remove my mugshot and fingerprints from their system.

As we left the courthouse, I shook Wade's hand and smiled. The journey had been hell but the outcome was splendid. And it was in large part all because of my lawyer.

The happiness we felt over the positive end to my legal troubles was somewhat tempered by the peace bond conditions I would have to live under and the inevitable media induced backlash that we knew would happen on the local forum and on social media.

I was not found guilty of any crime but it felt like I had been punished during the two and a half years it took for a resolution to my court case to play out. It's a wonder we didn't break as we waited and waited for one court date or one trial date after another to come and go. Adjournments gave us no hope; they accentuated the hopelessness we felt at times.

For one more year, I would not be completely free to do as I wanted as the peace bond was in effect. The conditions were not so much punitive as they were cautionary. I got that although the conditions didn't seem to take into account that the whole, ugly mess I found myself in had its roots in a mental disorder.

I was not a danger to children. Never had been. The charges that had been filed against me had never been about children. Nevertheless, I had to stay away from young people under the age of 19 for a year. That would mostly be easy to accomplish but it put a big question mark over future job prospects if I were to come into contact with a young person alone.

Understandably, I had to stay away from peer-to-peer communications under the peace bond. It was a certain piece of peer-to-peer software that allowed me to chat to an undercover police officer and clearly the court would want me to refrain from doing so.

The peace bond also stipulated that I partake in activities that are more benign for the next year, including continuing to take my medications, stay away from all forms of pornography and participate in any counselling as deemed necessary.

I also had to report to a probation officer, who would meet with me at regular intervals to see how I was doing.

The conditions also seemed a bit silly in the end given that, for two and a half years since the police showed up at my door with a search warrant, I was free to do as I wanted and I had no conditions to follow.

There was no question that I would fully comply with the conditions. Overall, they would not overtly affect my ability to live a peaceful life and they were a darn sight better than facing six months or more in jail. I had to accept them and be determined to adhere to every condition for a period of one year.

Because there were two reporters in the courtroom, there were quickly two reports circulating about the outcome of my legal case. That spawned a whole raft of articles on websites and in newspapers, which inevitably meant the anonymous, armchair quarterbacks of the local forum and on social media piped in with their negative, abusive and irrelevant comments.

Why Jackie and I bothered to read the comments I don't know. We did and they initially depressed us. The comments focussed on how it was perceived that I got a slap on the wrist. Several posters commented that it was unseemly for Jackie and I to high-five each other in the courtroom. Apparently, our elation at the end of our ordeal was not perceived very well.

I contemplated going on the forum and setting the record straight but I quickly came to realize I needn't bother. Some of the people posting about me were kind and supportive. The few people who did rant were childish, abusive and hiding behind anonymity and they just weren't worth the effort to try to correct. It didn't matter that half of what they wrote was utter bullshit. Perhaps they had their own mental health issues to contend with and one thing I had learned is not to judge people when they have serious issues of their own.

The local paper published an excellent article on the outcome of my court case. The local reporter was the only reporter brave enough to contact me and ask for an interview. I granted it. I knew the paper was going to publish something so why not give some input toward the hope that the article would be on the truthful side.

OCD was at the core of the local paper's article. The reporter did a great job describing how OCD is not what people think it is and she delved into the type of the disorder I had that got me into trouble. It was a report more about a mental health issue than it was about a distasteful legal case. I was grateful for the article and how it was written.

For nearly 40 years, I suffered from Obsessive Compulsive Disorder. It started soon after my dad died on a frozen Alberta highway and continued past the day the police showed up at my door with a search warrant.

I suffered from intense, intrusive thoughts of driving headlong into oncoming traffic, thinking I stole chocolate bars at checkout counters, afraid of being gay, having to do A before B happened, rape, maiming, killing, children and sex and a host of others. For most of my life, I had no idea what the thoughts meant or why I was getting them. And I kept it all a secret from the ones I loved.

My life changed the day I walked into a psychiatrist's office. He proclaimed I had OCD, that I had suffered enough and that all the bad thoughts I had were because of the disorder.

I was put on medications, I went to a relaxation course, I attended Cognitive Behavioral Therapy classes, and I became very educated about OCD. I did everything I could to improve my situation and with a lot of hard work I became more than my disorder.

With the end of suffering from OCD, I could have said goodbye to the disorder. I could have washed my hands of having to do anything with it and got on with a life free from the ravages of it.

But I didn't.

From the moment I started getting better, I became interested in the plight of other sufferers. I started working on a book that it might help other sufferers. I logged onto the OCD-UK forum and began giving advice to people who were lost, confused and sometimes hopeless. I started my own website, www.ocdlife.ca, so I could have a place to blog about the disorder and how to effectively deal with it.

I became invested in other sufferers. I wanted other people to get better. I wanted them to learn and to have hope.

Just as Jackie turned on the porch light so I could find my way home on my darkest day, I could shine a light for sufferers so they could find their way to wellness. By writing a book, talking to people, writing blog posts and answering questions on forums I could show a light to people I feel a kinship to. Maybe with my help, they could find their way.

For the longest time I thought I overcame OCD. I told people I overcame my disorder and I told people on the OCD-UK forum that if they worked hard they could overcome their disorder. It sounded good but it wasn't really the truth.

Overcome brings with it the concept of cure. Cure, when you think about it, means everything is fixed and no more intervention is needed to stay that way. But I realized that isn't where I ended up.

I continued to take two different medications at regular, 12-hour intervals, seven days a week. If I were suddenly to stop taking medications, I have no doubt the OCD would be back with a vengeance.

I also continued to get intrusive thoughts. They weren't anywhere near as severe as they used to be but I still got them occasionally. That meant I had to put into practice, almost every day, what I had learned from Cognitive Behavioral Therapy.

Having OCD is, at least for me, like being an alcoholic. Once you're an alcoholic you're always an alcoholic, even when you don't drink. In that regard, I believe I will always have OCD. I was no longer a sufferer because I no longer suffered from it but OCD was still a part of me and likely always will be.

I came to see that instead of talking of overcoming OCD, I came to a point, through medications and therapy, where I managed my OCD very well. It's more like I was facing a wild tiger and, with a chair and a whip, I tamed the tiger. I tamed OCD. I brought it down to its knees and made it a pathetic version of itself. It no longer affected me, but it was still there, lurking in the background.

I have OCD. I always will. I control it. It does not control me.

I walked alone down a dark path that no one knew I was

taking. I was urged forward by a mental disorder that battered my resolve, raped my sense of self and killed my motivation. My mind was assaulted with a barrage of thoughts and images so horrifying and evil that they usurped my self-image and left me believing I was sick and twisted.

In the real world, I managed to survive, just barely. There was little of myself to give to others and I felt completely unworthy of the support and love from others. I was trapped in a hell I could not change or control and that negatively affected every aspect of my life.

I was lost.

Bombarded by relentless intrusive thoughts, I took solace in the desolate realm of mental compulsions. In my mind, I fought against the thoughts with more thoughts. Not only did the compulsions not do any good, but also they fed the mental disorder, causing even more intrusive thoughts to appear.

I chatted on the Internet because of a twisted, compulsive urge. Decades of being pummelled by gruesome thoughts of children and sex convinced me that I was a pedophile, that I was capable of harm to children and that I could find comfort in communicating my thoughts to others. It didn't work out that way. Far from comfort, I found instead torment – the same anguish I suffered from intrusive thoughts.

Getting caught talking about an illegal subject was a duel-edged situation. My real life world was turned upside down and I was subjected to derision, contempt and disdain. My mental world became exposed and I could no longer keep it a secret. I sought help and through medications, therapy and the love and support of my family and friends, I got better. I became mentally healthy for the first time in nearly 40 years.

Where charges of child pornography would have destroyed a lesser marriage, love, compassion and understanding strengthened the bond between Jackie and me.

With my healthier mind comes a resolve to help others who have found themselves caught in the ravages of Obsessive Compulsive Disorder. Whatever the future holds, it will include assisting sufferers who find themselves lost and alone.

OCD beat me up. It damn near killed me. I fought back and put the disorder in its place. I survived. Then I went past survival and I lived, as I never had before.

About the author

Dave Preston is an author, freelance writer and small town journalist. *Truth Be Told: A journey from the dark side of OCD* is his first book. He lives in British Columbia's Okanagan Valley with his wife Jackie, his son and the indelible memory of Miss Kitty.

You can help

If you enjoyed this book, if it changed your mind about what OCD is, if it made you think deeply, won't you consider logging onto your favorite online book retailer and leaving a review? It both helps the author and helps other readers discover this book.

Connect Online

www.OCDLife.ca
www.twitter.com/ocdlife

Printed in Great Britain
by Amazon